ICNC **MONOGRAPH** SERIES

SERIES EDITOR: Maciej Bartkowski
CONTACT: mbartkowski@nonviolent-conflict.org
VOLUME EDITOR: Amber French
DESIGNED BY: David Reinbold
CONTACT: icnc@nonviolent-conflict.org

Other volumes in this series:

The Tibetan Nonviolent Struggle: A Strategic and Historical Analysis, Tenzin Dorjee (2015)

Published by ICNC Press
International Center on Nonviolent Conflict
1775 Pennsylvania Ave. NW
Suite 1200
Washington, D.C. 20006 USA

© 2015 International Center on Nonviolent Conflict, Juan Masullo
All rights reserved. ISBN: 978-1-943271-04-7

Cover photos: (l) Author, (r) D. Fellous/Colombia Tierra Herida/Vivero. Title page: Luis Benavides / The Associated Press

Left: This sign in the Peace Community of San José de Apartadó reads: "I am happy when the community struggles" in Spanish.

Right: San José de Apartadó, February 19, 2010. PCSJA members are marching while holding photos of the February 21, 2005 massacre victims.

Title page: A man carrying his bed leaves San José de Apartadó after the Colombian government opened a police outpost there in 2005. As this decision went clearly against the will of the PCSJA and overtly violated the *raison d'être* of neutrality, PCSJA members that year relocated a few miles away to the hamlet of La Holandita. For the PCSJA, relocation was a strategic nonviolent action through which the battlefield was rearranged to avoid both displacement and compromising neutrality. Today, a decade after the relocation, most of the members live in La Holandita and La Union, east of San José center. Despite violence and impunity, the Community has existed since 1997 and remains firm in its determination to nonviolently resist war today.

The designations used and material presented in this publication do not indicate the expression of any opinion whatsoever on the part of ICNC. The author holds responsibility for the selection and presentation of facts contained in this work, as well as for any and all opinions expressed therein, which are not necessarily those of ICNC and do not commit the organization in any way.

The Power of Staying Put:

NONVIOLENT RESISTANCE AGAINST ARMED GROUPS IN COLOMBIA

Abstract

In irregular civil wars, armed groups strategically aim to conquer, preserve and control territories. Local civilians inhabiting these territories respond in a wide variety of forms. Although the two dominant responses seem to be to collaborate with the strongest actor in town or flee the area, civilians are not stuck with only these choices. Collectively defying armed groups by engaging in organized nonviolent forms of noncooperation, self-organization and disruption is another option. However, given the huge disproportionality of force, it is still unclear why ordinary unarmed civilians choose to defy fully armed opponents, let alone how they manage to coordinate and act collectively, and even achieve results that often go against the strategic interests of the armed groups.

This monograph examines this puzzle through a detailed case study of one instance of sustained and organized civil resistance led by ordinary peasants against state and non-state repressive actors in Colombia's longstanding civil war: the case of the Peace Community of San José de Apartadó (PCSJA).[1] Building on interview and archival material collected during fieldwork, a dataset on civilian victimization, and secondary literature, this monograph describes and analyzes the emergence of the PCSJA, focusing on the key choices made to launch its civil resistance campaign; the methods of nonviolent action used; the evolution of peasants' preference for nonviolent organizing and noncooperation; and the capacity for collective action. An improved knowledge of this form of civil resistance can serve as a solid basis for the diffusion of these strategies both in other areas of Colombia and abroad, as well as for the design of post-conflict reconstruction strategies.

---

[1] I am immensely grateful to the Peace Community of San José de Apartadó and residents of nearby villages for sharing with me their experiences, inviting me to visit them and hosting me in their hamlets during my fieldwork trips. What I have learned from and with them is just incommensurable. I would also like to thank the Fellowship for Reconciliation (FOR) and Operazione Colomba for helping me get in touch with the Community, and Diego Gambetta, Bela Greskovits, Donatella della Porta, Sidney Tarrow and Elisabeth Wood for helping me carry out the larger project this monograph is part of and guiding me through the intricacies of field research in conflict-affected areas. Last but not least, I am grateful to ICNC, especially to Maciej Bartkowski and Amber French for their support, edits and comments throughout the elaboration of this monograph.

Table of Contents

Abstract 4
Introduction 7
    The Puzzle 9
    Research Questions and Objectives 9
    The Structure 10
Chapter 1: Literature Review 11
    Social Movements/Contentious Politics and the Study of Violence 13
    Civil War Studies and the Study of Civilian Agency 15
    Civil Resistance and the Study of Civil War 16
Chapter 2: Conceptualizing Civil Resistance in Civil War 19
Chapter 3: The Creation of the PCSJA 23
    Local and Regional Dynamics of a National War 23
    The Decision to Stay 29
    The Choice of Nonviolent Methods 31
    Guiding Principles and Organizational Structure 33
    Armed Groups' Reaction and the PCSJA Response 40
Chapter 4: The Emergence of the PCSJA: Identifying Explanatory Factors 43
    The Preference for Noncooperation: Violence that Stimulated Nonviolent Resistance .. 43
    The Capacity to Resist 48
    Prior Experiences of Collective Action 48
    The Role of External Actors 49
Chapter 5: Civil Resistance: The Methods of Nonviolent Action 51
    Disruptive Actions 51
    Contained Actions 54
    Routinized Actions 55
    Internationalized Actions: The Struggle Beyond Borders 55
    Tactics of the PCSJA's Nonviolent Struggle 58
Chapter 6: Conclusion: Lessons from the PCSJA 69
    For External Actors Willing to Support a Resisting Community as an Accompanier 70
    For Policymakers Working to Bring Peace in War-Torn Countries 72
Cited Literature 76
Acronyms 87
List of Figures 88

Introduction

*I*n March 1997, after the violent incursion of right-wing counter-insurgent paramilitary armies into San José, a rural village in northwestern Colombia, unarmed civilians responded to escalating armed conflict by taking a stand against war and declaring themselves neutral. They publicly committed not to participate directly or indirectly in the war, not to provide any strategic or material goods to any armed group, and not to carry weapons or allow others to carry them in the areas they inhabited. By doing so, they established the Peace Community of San José de Apartadó (PCSJA), an experiment of civilian-led nonviolent resistance that, despite violent repression from state and non-state armed groups, still persists today. Beyond San José, civilians in villages in Colombia and abroad have engaged in similar forms of contentious collective action to resist armed groups' strategies.

Facing acute violence from various armed groups fighting over the control of their village, San José residents found themselves in a situation characterized by a sense of under-protection and uncertainty about their destinies. It was survival that was at stake: "In reality, [armed groups] were killing people almost every day. Those who had to go down [to Apartadó] used to say 'I will go to Apartadó, but I don't know if I will make it back.' And it was always like this; if it was not women, it was men."[2] San José peasants had to make a choice between staying put in the village, thus risking to get killed at any time, or leave their lands behind, thus having to try their luck somewhere else in the country or abroad.

Fear, under-protection and uncertainty pushed many people to leave their rural village and find their way to other places, mainly one of the two major cities in the region, Apartadó (the capital of the Municipality of Apartadó) and Medellín (the capital of the Department of Antioquia). Flight is indeed a common reaction to fear, but 'fighting' back is another possible response (Elster 1999): several families decided to stay put.

---

[2] Interview L(G)/PCSJA#7 25.04.2014
Interview data is cited in footnotes, with ID number and data when the interview was conducted. Interviewees are identified with ID number (#) in order to ensure anonymity and confidentiality. L stands for leader; P for peasant; IA for international accompaniment; and E for external actors. G denotes group interview. All citations from interviews were translated into English by the author.

However, their choice for not leaving—forcefully or voluntarily[3]—was, by necessity, one that included the search for ways to not get killed for remaining in place (Anderson and Wallace 2012, 142). As one interviewee put it: "It was the violence that took place at that time which made people resist."[4] After intense deliberation, first among villagers and later with external actors, San José residents reached the conclusion that to resist displacement they needed to act collectively, to coordinate and organize themselves to develop a set of behavioral rules of noncooperation that could disrupt 'business-as-usual' for violent actors.

Therefore, the families who stayed decided to congregate in San José center, a place that was almost a ghost town after most of its residents fled. San José was a convenient location as it had enough room for hosting people from other hamlets and was, at the same time, close enough for people to return to their hamlets as soon as they could. For many, moving to San José was not simply considered displacement; on the contrary, it was seen as part of a strategy to avoid it. As one interviewee stated: "We stayed here because of the land. If we left, we wouldn't know if we could come back to our lands later on. Knowing that we can work on our land here, it was better to stay even if it was the most painful thing to do. That was our idea, not to go far away because from here [San José center] we could go and work our lands."[5]

Constantly hiding from armed groups and struggling everyday with hunger and disease, those who stayed held meetings to discuss possibilities and explore organizational forms. Building on existing community leadership and know-how from previous experiences of collective action, and with the important support of national and international nongovernmental organizations (NGOs) and religious organizations, peasants of San José declared themselves neutral to a war they did not feel was theirs and established an organized space, liberated from violence, in the middle of war.

---

[3] It is important to note that many villagers had to stay in San José because they had nowhere else to go or no money to move somewhere else. The way one leader described how villagers from her hamlet responded holds for most of my interviewees: "Well, people left. Some families went to Apartadó, others left to Bogotá, or different places in the country. And others, we stayed because we did not have a place to go." Interview L/PCSJA#8 26.04.2014

[4] Interview P/PCSJA#37 02.06.2014

[5] Interview P/PCSJA#14 29.04.2014

Introduction

The Puzzle

The risk involved in challenging violent armed groups is extraordinarily high, and there is uncertainty about the prospects of success. In addition, it is not at all clear why unarmed civilians choose to resist heavily armed groups in the midst of civil war. Material interests, expected benefits resulting directly from participation, selective incentives and the widening of political opportunities and/or narrowing of threats (Goldstone and Tilly 2001; McAdam 1982; Olson 1965; Popkin 1979)—all central elements in conventional explanations of collective action—do not provide a complete, convincing account of the emergence of these resisting communities. Contrary to what some theories would predict, civilians have had cogent and enduring motives to participate in nonviolent resistance against armed groups' strategies in their localities.

Research Question and Objectives

This monograph deals with ordinary civilians and the nonviolent collective roles they come to play during civil war. The story it tells is one of war, violence and suffering, but also one of solidarity, organization and courage. It aims to offer a detailed account of the forces that pushed San José de Apartadó villagers into civil resistance, and closely describe and analyze the process of launching their civil resistance campaign. Although it touches on issues related to how civil resistance is advanced and sustained in a warzone and the outcomes it can yield, the monograph focuses on the emergence of the PCSJA. Contextual and strategic factors are described and analyzed to improve readers' understanding of the choices that San José villagers made.

More broadly speaking, this monograph seeks to provide an initial response to the questions, why do some unarmed civilians choose to nonviolently resist armed groups in the midst of civil war? How do they decide to organize themselves? How do they succeed in resisting without arms despite adversarial conditions?

The Structure

The monograph is structured in seven sections. Following the introduction, the second section presents a brief review of the three main bodies of literature on which this study builds, identifying both the opportunities they offer and the gaps to be filled. The third section conceptualizes civil resistance in the context of civil war, locating it within a wider portfolio of possible responses civilians have when facing lasting presence of armed groups in their territories. The fourth section describes in detail how the PCSJA was created, presenting an overview of the local and regional contexts in which the Community was set up. This section addresses some of the main choices villagers had to make to launch their campaign, introduces their guiding principles and internal organizational structure, and outlines the immediate reaction of armed groups and how villagers responded. The fifth section identifies and elaborates on some key factors that help explain the emergence of the PCSJA, focusing on the evolution of a desire for noncooperation and the capacity of villagers to collectively act upon it. The sixth section deals with the methods of nonviolent action that villagers used to set up the Community and on which they have relied to run and advance their struggle. The monograph closes with lessons drawn from the case study which can be useful for NGO actors and policy communities.

Chapter 1
Literature Review

Civilian support in civil war settings has been commonly identified as indispensable for the advancement of armed groups' strategic objectives and even for their survival (Wickham-Crowley 1987). Consequently, civilian collaboration with and participation in armed groups has been widely explored in both civil war and social movement literatures (Bosi and Della Porta 2012; Humphreys and Weinstein 2008; Kalyvas 2006; Viterna 2006; Viterna 2013; Wood 2003). Nevertheless, evidence from warzones shows that those who actively (and voluntarily) support armed groups beyond a coerced minimum, or join their ranks as full- or part-time members constitute a minority of the entire population caught up in war.[6] It follows that the portfolio of possible civilian responses to war pressures is not limited to different kinds and/or degrees of cooperation with armed actors. This begs the question, what do those who do not join or support armed groups do when inhabiting a warzone?

Various bodies of literature have partially tackled this question. Studies in wartime migration point to one aspect: that many civilians flee to other locations either in the same country or abroad. A cursory look at available data on displacement and refugees would suffice to confirm that in civil wars a considerable number of civilians flee from their localities (Adhikari 2012, 2013; Engel and Ibáñez 2007; Ibáñez 2009; Steele 2009a, 2011). However, the question of what those who stay put do has not been addressed in wartime migration literature and warrants further research (Adhikari 2013, 88).

Scholars interested in militias, armed village guards, civil defense forces and the like have provided another part of the answer: some civilians join together to counter armed groups with organized violence of their own (Francis 2005; Hoffman 2004; Hoffman 2007). Finally, scholars studying the micro-dynamics of civil war have discussed, although not in detail, the (unlikely) possibility that civilians follow individual self-help

---

[6] For example, Lichbach (1995, 8) estimated that active participants in rebellion account for only about 5 percent of the population, while Wood (2003) found in her study of insurgent collective action in El Salvador that civilian participation fell below one-third in the areas where she conducted research.

strategies such as double-dealing or fence-sitting (i.e. simultaneous defection towards both sides, helping both sides at the same time, *attentisme*) (Kalyvas 2006, 225–235).

With research to date, we know a great deal about civilian cooperation and displacement, have important insights about organized armed resistance, and count on some basic intuitions about nonviolent responses at the individual level. However, when it comes to organized forms of nonviolent civil resistance in the context of civil war, we still know very little. To be sure, some scholars, practitioners and activists have documented instances in which civilians have collectively and nonviolently responded to armed group pressures in different places afflicted by war.[7] This work provides valuable case studies and useful conceptual tools which have informed this monograph. However, nonviolent resistance in civil wars, such as the campaign advanced by the PCSJA, has not yet been systematically explored in the scholarly literature, let alone theorized. As a result,

> *The portfolio of possible civilian responses to war pressures is not limited to different kinds and/or degrees of cooperation with armed actors. This begs the question, what do those who do not join or support armed groups do when inhabiting a warzone?*

we still know very little about the conditions under which nonviolent resistance is more likely to emerge and/or be sustained over time, the different forms it is likely to take and the determinants of its variation, and the outcomes it is likely to yield, among other unknowns. Without this improved knowledge, the task of drawing specific recommendations for people willing to support such communities or transfer good practices somewhere else will be speculative rather than grounded in practice and reality.

From a conceptual and theoretical point of view, civil war, social movement and civil resistance are the three main bodies of research which inform this study. While scholars in these subfields have made important contributions, their work has evolved in separate trajectories and few attempts to link these bodies of literature have been

---

[7] For accounts of experiences in other places in the world see: Mozambique (Anderson and Wallace 2012; Perlez 1990; Wilson 1991; Wilson 1992); the Philippines (Avruch and Jose 2007; Garcia 1997; Santos 2005); Uganda (Baines and Paddon 2012); Afghanistan, Bosnia and Rwanda (Anderson and Wallace 2012); and Colombia (Anderson and Wallace 2012; Bouvier 2009; Hernandez Delgado 2004; Mitchell and Ramírez 2009; Mitchell and Rojas 2012; Rojas 2007; Sanford 2003; Sanford 2004; Uribe 2004).

made.[8] In this monograph, I hope to show that a sustained dialogue between these three specialized literatures can improve our social scientific understanding of civilian behavior in civil war, collective organizing in high-risk settings, and strategic nonviolent actions undertaken against repressive actors. In what follows, I identify the opportunities and shortcomings that each body of work has with regard to the study of nonviolent resistance in civil war.

Social Movements/Contentious Politics and the Study of Violence

From different theoretical perspectives, students of social movements have shown that context has a decisive impact on the emergence, trajectories, performances and outcomes of contentious collective action. However, due to the field's long bias towards the study of Western parliamentary democracies and reformist movements in relatively safe and peaceful environments, this literature has not yet explored collective action in civil war settings systematically.[9] After several pleas to expand the geographical and thematic frontiers of the field, some work was advanced on phenomena relevant to the study of civil resistance in civil war: the issue of repression increasingly captured the attention of scholars in the field and, more generally, the study of political violence was placed in the wider context of strategies of action and cycles of protest.[10] This move made the examination of the relationships between violent and nonviolent strategies in both violent and nonviolent contexts possible.

---

[8] In fact, scholars from all three subfields have condemned this lack of dialogue and the 'cordial indifference' in which these bodies of work have proceeded. McAdam, Tarrow and Tilly, individually and collectively, have called our attention to the lack of dialogue between students of different forms of contentious politics (see McAdam, Tarrow, and Tilly 2001). More concretely, Tarrow (forthcoming; 2007; 2011) has called attention to the segmentation between students of violent phenomena and social movement scholars; Schock (2005, xviii–xix), Smithey and Kurtz (2003) and Lipsitz and Kritzer (1975, 729) to the lack of dialogue between political process literature (or political protest more generally) and studies on nonviolent action; and finally, Chenoweth and Cunningham (2013, 272–274) to the lack of dialogue between literatures on violent conflict and on civil resistance.

[9] This prolonged neglect is indeed surprising, as already in the mid-1980s a prominent scholar in the field, Doug McAdam (1986) suggested and illustrated in a detailed case study of the Mississippi Freedom Summer that the dynamics of high-risk collective action were likely to be qualitatively different from those where risks are low or nonexistent.

[10] For recent reviews of how social movements have approached the study of political violence and the topics that this literature has privileged see della Porta (2008) and *Mobilization's* Special Issue on Political Violence and Terrorism edited by Goodwin (2012). For reviews and critical assessments of how repression has been treated in social movements research see Earl (2003; 2004; 2006).

However, despite a long tradition of work stressing civilian agency, this literature has failed to capture nonviolent civilian agency in civil wars within their research net for at least three reasons. First, movement scholars have seldom taken seriously the specific dynamics and processes that define the institutional setting of civil war; for example, when comparing violent settings to nonviolent ones, civil wars have been frequently lumped together with other "repressive" or "violent" situations such as authoritarian or semi-authoritarian regimes. In addition, efforts to provide typologies of political violence (Bosi and Malthaner 2013; Della Porta 1995; Tilly 2003) and/or to identify general mechanisms that travel across different types of violent settings (McAdam, Tarrow, and Tilly 2001; Tilly 2003), although valuable for other purposes, have been too general in their scope to increase our understanding of the nitty-gritty of nonviolent collective action in the midst of civil war violence. This general scope proves less useful when it comes to guiding policy or providing specific recommendations for practitioners willing to stimulate such campaigns in other civil war settings or to support already existing ones.

Second, the emphasis on violent interactions and actors has prevented scholars from examining what happens with those who remain in a warzone, and who neither engage in violent acts nor are mere bystander victims or resources to be plundered. It is precisely these individuals who can become empowered agents of change.[11] Third, by reproducing the state-centered perspective common to social movement studies in which governance units are limited to state institutions, their representatives or elites (Della Porta 2008, 224; Earl 2006, 129; Goldstone forthcoming), this literature has failed to identify non-state actors, such as armed groups, as agents of *de facto* authority, control and repression. For that matter, as with civil wars, the centers of authority are multiplied and extend beyond the state realm, as too are the actors that ordinary people may wish to resist.[12]

---

[11] This bias is clearly reflected in the menu of topics that have captured most of the attention in this body of literature: e.g., escalation and radicalization processes, states' violent responses to dissenters, the policing of protest, mobilization/demobilization into/from violent groups, resource mobilization for violent organizations, radical flank effects, outcomes of political violence and narratives of violence, among others.

[12] In recent revisions of the contentious politics program, there has been a shift away from this tendency by using more general terms that go beyond the state, such as "elites, authorities or other contentious actors" (see Tarrow forthcoming). Furthermore, forthcoming work in the field of social movement studies is questioning not only the centrality of the state in conventional models of social movements, but also the potentially misleading tendency to treat it as a unitary actor (see Duyvendak and Jasper forthcoming).

Chapter 1: Literature Review

Civil War Studies and the Study of Civilian Agency

Students of civil war have recently shifted their focus away from questions of macro processes such as civil war onset, duration, termination and recurrence.[13] A new interest in the local dynamics of civil wars on the ground, with a focus on the concrete behavior of individuals, households and communities living in warzones, has captured the attention of several civil war scholars.[14] Following Kalyvas' (2003, 481) observation that civilians "cannot be treated as passive, manipulated, or invisible actors", researchers have included the role of civilians in their description, conceptualization and theorization of several civil war dynamics.

Although these studies have undoubtedly pointed our attention to civilian agency and civil war social processes,[15] the core of the work has focused on the "more salacious aspects of insurgents interactions with civilians" (Mampilly 2011, 6). In consequence, "nonviolent activities have been particularly overlooked by the political science literature aiming to understand how armed groups behave, how civilians make choices in the midst of war, and what the long-term consequences of these encounters are" (Arjona forthcoming, chap. 1). We need a more direct insight into the broader set of interactions that armed groups constantly engage in with civilians, as well as into the different ways in which these communities respond to armed groups' strategies.

In the last few years, some scholars have taken a fundamental step towards the systematic study of this broader set of armed group-civilian interactions by examining armed groups' governance and social order. Ana Arjona, Nelson Kasfir and Zachariah Mampilly have advanced our understanding of the nonviolent ways in which armed groups approach civilians in the areas they control and aim to govern (such as the provision of goods and services), as well as how civilian responses can shape armed groups' behavior (Arjona forthcoming b; Arjona 2013; Kasfir 2005; Mampilly 2011). In

---

[13] For recent, extensive reviews of this literature focusing on macro-processes see Blattman and Miguel (2010), Cederman, Gleditsch, and Buhaug (2013, chap. 2).

[14] For promises and pitfalls of this research program, see Kalyvas (2008). For a recent refining and extension of one of its basic and most influential models (the Control-Collaboration Model), see Kalyvas (2012). Additionally, see the *Journal of Conflict Resolution's* special issue on "Disaggregating Civil War" edited by Cederman and Gleditsch (2009); the *Journal of Peace Research's* special issue on the micro-level analysis of violent conflict edited by Verwip, Justino and Brück (2009); an edited volume by these three same scholars (Justino, Brück, and Verwimp 2014); and the *Journal of Conflict Resolution's* special issue on "Bridging Micro and Macro Approaches on Civil Wars and Political Violence" edited by Balcells and Justino (2014).

[15] For a discussion of what constitutes a social process in civil war, see Wood (2008a).

particular, Arjona (forthcoming b) has begun to theorize instances of civilian resistance against armed groups' rule and how this type of response is likely to shape the type of social order that emerges. In addition to work in rebel governance and social orders, studies exploring civilian protection (Valenzuela 2009; Valenzuela 2010) and civilian autonomy (Kaplan 2010; Kaplan 2012; Kaplan 2013) have begun to explore more systematically the dynamics that are very closely related to what this monograph conceptualizes as civilian-based nonviolent resistance.

Civil Resistance and the Study of Civil War

As mentioned above, both civil war studies and social movement research in areas afflicted by violence have been dominated by concerns about violent dynamics and violent groups. Although there are logical and compelling reasons for this focus, it obscures the crucial fact that even in contexts that are largely characterized by the widespread use of violence, violence is not the only form of collective organizing we observe, let alone necessarily the most effective. The blooming body of work on civil resistance has clearly evidenced this fact.[16]

Not until very recently have students of civil resistance moved beyond the mainly applied, historical, descriptive and sometimes normative approach that predominated early scholarship on nonviolent action (e.g., Ackerman and DuVall 2000; Bartkowski 2013; Holmes and Gan 2005; Sharp 1973, 2003, 2005) and begun to analyze these occurrences from a more empirical, theory-informed and analytical perspective (Chenoweth and Stephan 2011; Nepstad 2011; Schock 2005; Svensson and Lindgren 2011). By stressing the role of unarmed, organized, ordinary actors in bringing about social and political change, this growing body of work sheds important light on the role that organized unarmed civilians can play in the midst of violence, including civil war settings.

This literature highlights civilian agency and stresses the strategic dimension and effectiveness of civil resistance actions even in the face of acute violence and when confronting heavily armed opponents. Instead of seeing civilians as victims, passive spectators of violence or holders of resources to be plundered, this literature

---

[16] Following a standard practice in this body of literature (see Chenoweth and Cunningham 2013, 273), I use 'civil resistance', 'nonviolent resistance', 'nonviolent struggle', 'strategic nonviolence', and 'nonviolent action' as synonyms and use them interchangeably (Bartkowski 2013a, 2; Chenoweth and Cunningham 2013, 273).

has underlined their role as agents of change. Equally important, with its focus on the pragmatic and strategic aspects of nonviolent action rather than on its moral and principled underpinnings, this scholarship provides invaluable tools for understanding the choice of nonviolent action. Unlike social movement scholars who have generally treated nonviolent action as part of a continuum that goes from conventional political action to nonviolent action to violent action, civil resistance scholars view it as an exclusive alternative and strategic choice made by unarmed actors to advance their struggle independently and often despite adversarial conditions (Schock 2013, 280). This different treatment has allowed civil resistance scholars to examine in more detail the empirical and analytical differences between waging strategic violent or nonviolent conflicts.

> *Nonviolent action is an exclusive alternative and strategic choice made by unarmed actors to advance their struggle independently and often despite adversarial conditions.*

However, for several reasons, this literature has not yet captured the type of civilian resistance that this monograph examines.[17] First of all, apart from some interesting preliminary insights about the different drivers of nonviolent campaigns and civil war onset (Chenoweth and Lewis 2013), this literature has not examined the particularities of civil war settings.[18] Some studies have included in their samples countries that have experienced a civil war, as it is the case for social movement studies on political violence. However, the focus has been too general to capture the specific nuances of civil war that shape the type of civil resistance examined here.

This lack of attention to the civil war context has been further deepened by the centrality this literature tends to give to the state or its agents,[19] its reliance on aggregate data, and its privileged focus on large-scale campaigns with maximalist goals. As with social movements/contentious politics scholarship, state-centrism has precluded scholars from capturing instances of nonviolent resistance that challenge *de facto* authorities other than the state (Masullo 2013). Aggregate data sacrifice important levels

---

[17] Kaplan's (2013) analysis of the Peasant Worker Association of the Carare River (ATCC) in Colombia is an important exception.

[18] Some work in this subfield has gone beyond the study of authoritarian regimes and autocracies in general and actually explored the specificities of some other violent contexts. The work of Semelin et. al (2011) is illustrative for the case of genocide.

[19] Civil resistance is generally defined as a popular challenge against a state relying on tactics that fall outside of the defined and accepted channels of the state (Chenoweth and Stephan 2011; Schock 2005; Svensson and Lindgren 2011).

of nuance (Chenoweth and Lewis 2013, 273), making it virtually impossible to capture instances of nonviolent action that take place at the subnational level in response to very local civil war dynamics. Furthermore, the focus on regime change, ending foreign occupations and/or secession has led scholars to overlook instances in which civilians, via village-level self-organizing, may pursue more micro—although similarly important and challenging—goals such as protection from violence or autonomy from armed groups and their rule.

Finally, while this monograph is concerned with the emergence of one instance of civil resistance, the literature has predominantly focused on explaining outcomes, devoting great effort to assess campaign success and failure. Although some of the main concepts, such as participation, resilience and leverage (Schock 2013, 282) are no doubt useful to assess the effectiveness of civil resistance strategies in civil war and/or to understand its duration over time, they do not help much to understand why it emerges and the variation in the form it takes.

Chapter 2
Conceptualizing Civil Resistance in Civil War

The subject of this monograph is nonviolent resistance in civil war. Nonviolent resistance is part of a wider portfolio of responses that civilians may use when living in a warzone. These responses are rarely fixed, as they are contingent upon both pre-war conditions and civil war dynamics. We thus see civilians adopting different roles in the course of war. In the changing environment of civil war, civilian strategies tend to shift over time. Therefore, when studying one set of responses, it is important to have in mind the different choices civilians have at their disposal when confronted by war.[20] Therefore, to conceptualize the type of response exhibited by the residents of San José de Apartadó, I locate their strategy of nonviolent resistance within a wider set of possibilities (Figure 1).[21]

---

[20] Theoretically, different courses of action are available to civilians living in warzones, and civilians are strategic actors who can provide or withdraw support to and from armed groups. However, this does not ignore the fact that their choices are constrained to varying degrees by the dynamics of war (see e.g., Weinstein 2007, 163). This monograph is cautious not to endorse a view of agency detached from the dynamics and processes that shape the institutional setting of a civil war and simplistically make civilians "authors of their own lives." As Gayer (2012) rightly observes in his study of female combatants in India, agents in civil wars are endowed with different capacities to amend the course of their lives.

[21] For a broader and more complex elaboration of civilian agency in civil wars, see Masullo (in progress).

Figure 1. **Civilian Responses to Civil War**

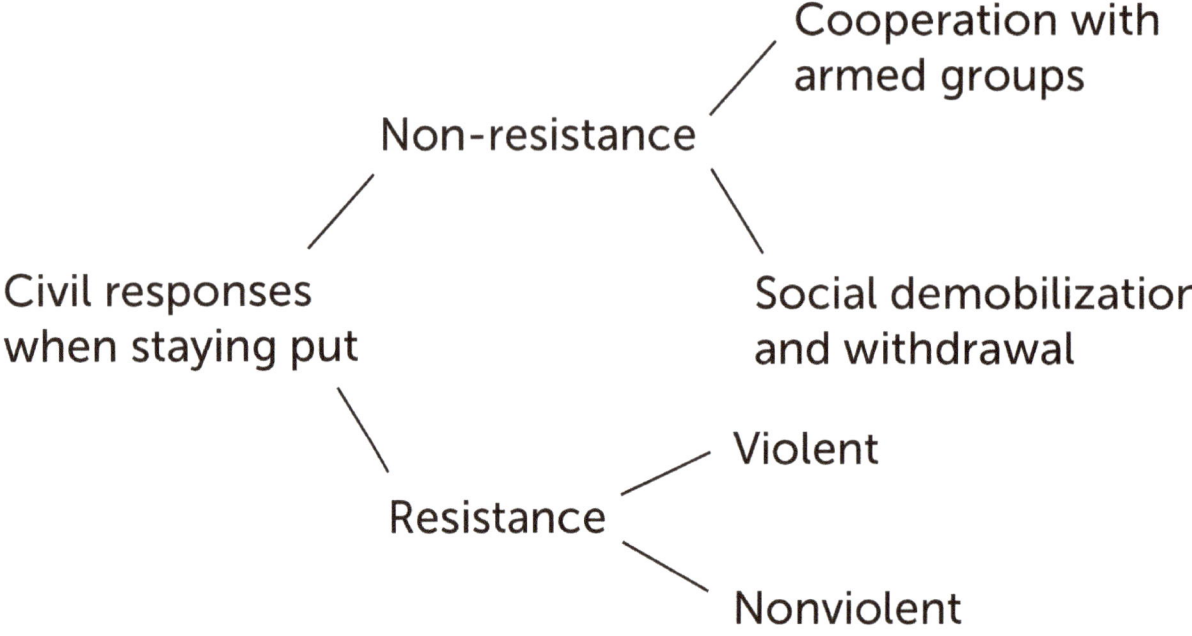

Source: Author

When armed groups establish a constant presence in a given locality, residents need to make choices about how to respond. If they stay put, they face two general courses of action regarding how to relate and interact with armed groups: they can opt for non-resistance or resistance. Broadly speaking, non-resistance comprises, on the one hand, of social demobilization and withdrawal to survive, and on the other hand, different forms of cooperation with armed groups. The behaviors that may count as cooperation can be divided into two broad types, both of which benefit armed groups in a direct way: obedience and support.[22] The former entails any civilian action that occurs in response to an order given by the armed group; the latter entails behaviors that civilians follow without being given any explicit or implicit order (Arjona, forthcoming: 38; 103-104).

---

[22] Different scholars have examined the range of civilian conduct that may count as cooperation and have analyzed it in their kind and degree (Arjona forthcoming a; Kalyvas 2006; Kasfir 2005; Viterna 2006; Viterna 2013; Weinstein 2007; Wood 2003). Although in the context of external occupation, Petersen (2001) and Gross (1979) provide examples of forms of cooperation that also inform civilian behavior in civil wars in meaningful ways.

The opposite of cooperation is resistance.[23] I follow the tradition in civil resistance studies and further divide resistance into violent and nonviolent forms.[24] Broadly speaking, resistance entails individual and collective instances of violent or nonviolent opposition to armed groups. The latter—nonviolent resistance—consists of acts of omission, commission or combinations of both. It comprises a wide range of behaviors that directly and/or indirectly affect armed groups' strategic interests (e.g. blocking access to survival goods or information resources). In this monograph, I deal with an instance of civil resistance that is collective, thus involving self-organizing by many, and nonviolent, thus relying on methods of nonviolent action. Finally, although nonviolent resistance can perfectly be deployed to serve a wider range of goals, in the case herein we are dealing with a group of peasants who, above all, organized themselves to seek protection from armed groups' violence.

Thus, the case of the PCSJA represents an instance of civilian-led nonviolent resistance in that:[25]

(i) The choice for organizing nonviolent resistance results from an autonomous decision taken by civilians and is deployed by them (i.e. it is civilian-led). That is to say, the nonviolent strategies advanced by San José villagers did not come 'from above' or 'from outside' the community, because external support was provided to the already planned or deployed action.

(ii) Nonviolent resistance brings resisters (San José villagers) and opponents (armed groups, including the national army and the police) into sustained

---

[23] Kalyvas (2006, 104) considers defection (i.e. active collaboration with the rival actor) to be the flipside of collaboration. Kalyvas & Kocher (2007) seem to reduce non-participation with armed groups to free riding or other non-collective behaviors. Steele (2009, 424) sees in the choice of staying a "strong signal that civilians will collaborate" with the stronger actor. However, as conceptualized here, when civilians opt to stay put, defect or not to participate in the conflict, their portfolio of individual and collective behaviors includes different options such as free riding, collaborating, or neither of the two.

[24] This distinction makes analytical sense, as violent forms of resistance are likely to present their own specific challenges and obstacles (such as finding arms, proper training, and overcoming moral barriers to the use of violence, among others), making it a phenomenon qualitatively different from that of nonviolent resistance. In fact, the dynamics of forming and/or participating in armed resistance are more likely to resemble those of participating in armed rebellion than those of self-organizing for nonviolent resistance (Arjona forthcoming a, chap 2; Chenoweth and Stephan 2011).

[25] In a broader project in progress, the PCSJA is included as one instance of what I call noncooperation in civil war. There I introduce the concept of noncooperation in civil war and establish a set of criteria for classifying cases and justify the reasons behind each criterion. See Masullo (in progress).

interaction. Thus, the PCSJA constitutes a campaign of civil resistance rather than just a set of sporadic and ephemeral acts of protest.

(iii)   The tactics used by San José villagers circumvent the conventional political channels for voicing demands established *de jure* by the Colombian state and *de facto* by armed groups. Thus, their nonviolent actions are not advanced through means that are accepted, let alone facilitated, by authorities. In other words, PCSJA's civil resistance campaign is non-institutional as it operates outside the bounds of institutionalized political channels (see Schock 2003, 705).

In sum, the PCSJA represents a type of political action or conflict led by ordinary civilians that relies on the use of various nonviolent methods and involves a range of sustained activities to challenge the oppressive structures established by armed groups present in the PCSJA locality. Above all, the experience of the PCSJA is a popular expression of the collective determination of villagers to self-organize and withdraw their cooperation from the powers of the armed groups in their locality (Bartkowski 2013a, 4-5; Roberts 2011, 2). Although they called themselves a Peace Community (in Spanish, *comunidad de paz*) and seldom refer to civil resistance or nonviolent resistance (in Spanish, *resistencia civil* or *resitencia noviolenta*) to describe what they do, villagers are in fact engaged in a process that constitutes civil or nonviolent resistance in both form and purpose.

Chapter 3
The Creation of the PCSJA

Local and Regional Dynamics of a National War

The Peace Community of San José de Apartadó is located in northwestern Colombia in the village of San José, municipality of Apartadó, department of Antioquia.[26] It is the first point of entry to the Abibe Mountains, the core of the Banana Axis, one of the five sub-regions comprising Urabá region (see Figure 2). The Urabá region is about one-tenth the land mass and population size of Colombia and is of great value for the country's commercial relations, agro-industrial activities and export economy. Moreover, it serves as a continental corridor between South and Central America via the Panama Canal and as a bridge connecting the departments of Córdoba, Chocó, and Antioquia in the Abibe Mountains. Due to its geographical and economic strategic value, Urabá quickly became one of the main stages of Colombia's ongoing civil war. Armed groups rapidly learned that whoever controls this area gains the military advantage of controlling a large portion of the country's northwest. Thus, apart from functioning as a pathway for smuggling arms and drugs, the Abibe Mountains became a rearguard zone for some of the strongest left-wing guerrilla groups in the country's war (Uribe 2004).

---

[26] Most of the hamlets of the PCSJA are located in the department of Antioquia, including downtown San José, where the villagers initially settled in 1997, and La Holandita, where they re-settled in 2005 after a police station was established in San José against their will, putting them at risk. More distant hamlets of the PCSJA are located in the neighboring department of Cordoba.

Figure 2. **Urabá in National, Regional and World Contexts**

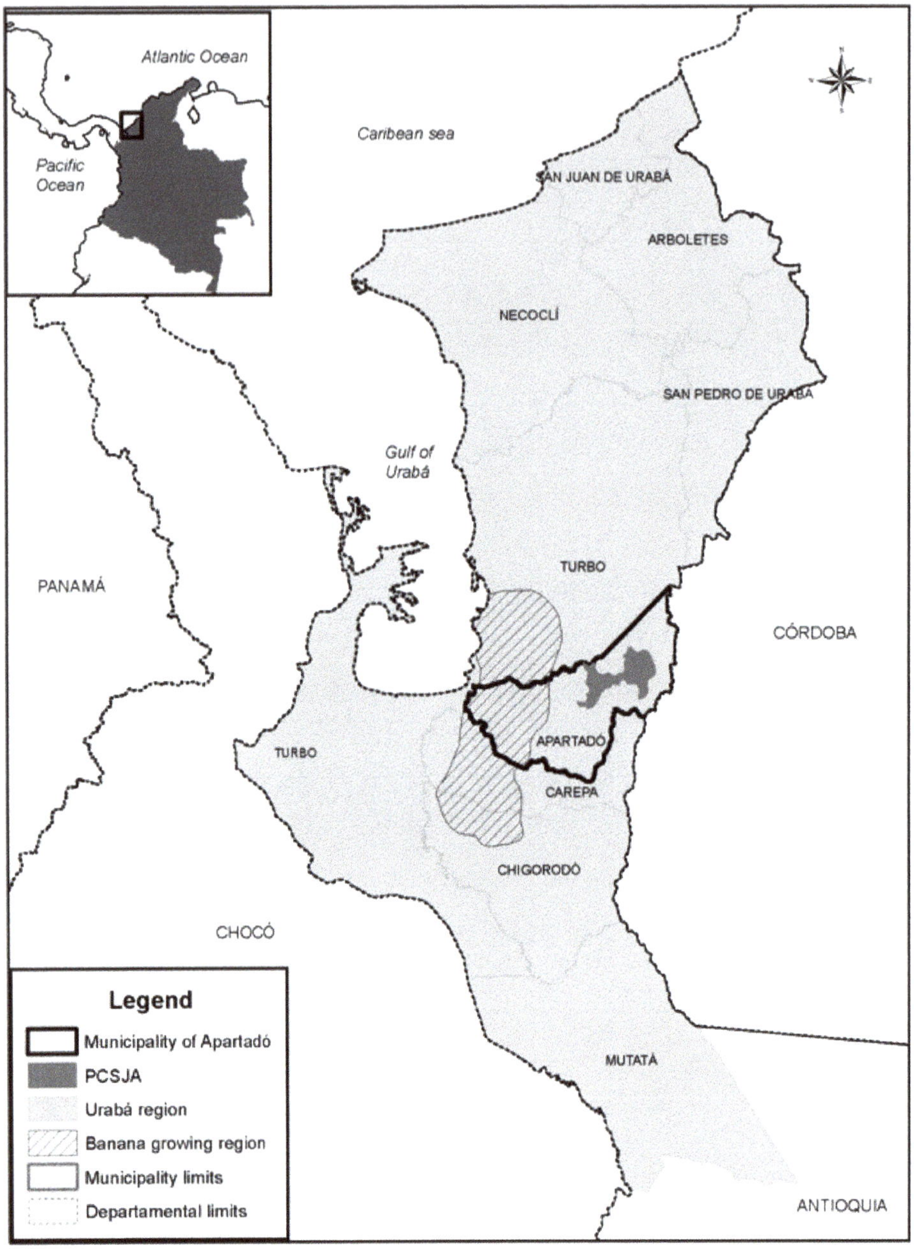

Source: Author[27]

---

[27] I am grateful to Maria Jose La Rota for her assistance in creating this map.

Chapter 3: The Creation of the PCSJA

Sparsely populated between the 1920s and the early 1950s, Urabá experienced an abrupt population increase in the late 1950s and 1960s as a result of the emerging agro-export banana industry, construction of new roads connecting it with important urban centers, and a large number of people fleeing from La Violencia.[28] This process attracted a large number of workers and led to a fast economic development and integration of the region. These transformations, however, were barely regulated by the state (Uribe 2004), leading to intense social and labor conflicts between banana plantation owners, large cattle ranchers (in some cases with strong ties to drug traffickers), trade unions, rural squatters and *campesino* (peasant) settlers (Carroll 2011). In this socially agitated context, several civic, communal and campesino associations emerged and trade unions were formed. Later, in the late 1960s and early 1970s, left-wing guerrilla groups emerged, permeating and radicalizing most of the already existing social and political movements (Bejarano 1988; Carroll 2011; Ramírez Tobón 1993; Restrepo 2011; Romero 2003).

Banana production has long been a staple in Urabá.
Photo source: Wikimedia Commons, Ramesh Ng

---

[28] Between 1951 and 1964 the population of Urabá increased by a factor of five, from 15,700 to 77,000 (Carroll 2011, 59). For a detailed account of the colonization process of Urabá and its intersections with the regional dynamics of violence, see Bejarano (1988).

The Popular Liberation Army (EPL) and the Revolutionary Armed Forces of Colombia (FARC) achieved considerable military capacity, established strong links with trade unions, and gained important social and political support from large portions of the population of Urabá.[29] However, in the late 1980s, Urabá experienced the violent incursion of paramilitary armies sponsored by local elites and drug traffickers. Although operating outside of the formal structures of the state, these groups operated in complicity with it (mainly with the national army and the police) or at least were highly tolerated in their task of neutralizing the advancement of guerrilla groups and any organized expression of the political left (Kalyvas and Arjona 2005; Romero 2000; Romero 2003).

The upending of alliances that followed the period of calm after the EPL demobilization in 1991 provided an opening for paramilitaries to dispute and finally conquer the area (Steele 2011, 431). Fidel and Carlos Castaño, two of the main leaders of what later became the largest paramilitary federation in the country, the United Self-Defense Forces of Colombia (AUC), commanded the main paramilitary group that operated in the region, the Campesino Self-Defense Forces of Córdoba and Urabá (ACCU).[30] In their strong military offensive to gain territorial control, the paramilitary armies disproportionately targeted civilians (see Figure 4 on page 44), aiming to kill them or strategically displace them in a process that came to be known as the "agrarian-counter reform" (Romero 2003; Steele 2011).[31] By 1997, the paramilitary armies managed to push the FARC to the geographical margins of the region and to submit both the village of San José and the city of Apartadó to their authority (Uribe 2004, 89).

After a long period of insurgent control by both the EPL and FARC during the

---

[29] The FARC, operating mainly in southern Urabá, established strong links with SINTRABANANO, a trade union of banana workers. Meanwhile the EPL, operating mainly in the north, established strong links with SINTAGRO, a trade union of agrarian workers (Carroll 2011).

[30] According to Stanford University's Mapping Militant Organization, the ACCU grew to become the largest contributor to the AUC, providing around 80 percent of its manpower nationwide. Although estimates of the size of the AUC vary substantially, after the Uribe administration came to terms with AUC in 2003 for a demobilization process, over 30,000 combatants were demobilized by 2008.

[31] Jairo Castillo (aka Pitirri), a former paramilitary leader serving as a key protected witness, described this strategy in the following terms: "It was a conspiracy. Some were doing the killing, others who would follow behind buying up the land, and a third wave who would legalize the new ownership of the land" (testimony presented by Iván Cepeda, Colombian human rights defender and Director of the National Movement for Victims of State Crimes [MOVICE], in August 2010 during a congressional debate on political control over land, paramilitaries and forced displacement).

Chapter 3: The Creation of the PCSJA

1970s and 1980s,[32] San José residents saw the arrival of paramilitaries in the mid-1990s. Multiple sources concur that 1996 was a critical juncture. In the words of a volunteer from the Fellowship of Reconciliation (FOR)[33] who worked with the Community for over six months: "[Everybody remembers] the 90s as one of conflict intensification, but if it is about one particular year, all will say it was 1996 with the definitive arrival of the paramilitaries."[34] On February 28, 1996, several San José residents were killed in a paramilitary roadblock installed at the entrance of the village. On August 16, unidentified armed men killed Bartolomé Cataño, the founder of San José, in the city of Apartadó, and two days later the paramilitaries killed Jorge Arias, a campesino who owned a small local shop that was also burned by the perpetrators. On August 29, members of the national army killed campesino Alberto Yepes in front of his wife and children. His body, as that of Orlando Usuga, another campesino killed in August, was falsely presented as that of a member of the guerrillas. On September 16, paramilitaries dragged four Community leaders out of their houses and killed them in front of a large group of residents (CINEP 2005; Uribe 2004; Zarate-Laun 2012).

While violence against civilians was comparatively low during insurgent control in the 1970s and 1980s,[35] it became more frequent in the 1990s where control was being disputed and two opposing sides clashed violently in the area. Compared to the times when paramilitaries were taking over, San Jose villagers recall the period of guerrilla control as a "peaceful" one: "Things were fine here. You could go out and work, you could do your things, you could live your life. The *guerrillos* [referring to the FARC] did not bother us; they were respectful and sometimes even tried to help us when the *paracos* [referring to the paramilitaries] came to harm us."[36] Throughout the 1980s

---

[32] The EPL controlled the western region of the municipality and the FARC controlled the village of San José, establishing themselves in the Abibe Mountains (Giraldo 2000; Suarez 2007). With EPL's demobilization in 1991, the FARC became the only guerrilla group operating in the area. As one interviewee noted, "With the demobilization of the EPL and before the arrival of the paramilitaries, the FARC carried out several state-like activities, such as providing protection, building roads, and supplying goods. Many residents of San José and hamlets nearby obeyed, actively collaborated with, and even joined the FARC during the 1980s and part of the 1990s. The FARC was the ruling authority." Interview IA/PCSJA#2 04.2012

[33] According to FOR's website: "Since 1915, the Fellowship of Reconciliation (FOR) has carried on programs and educational projects concerned with domestic and international peace and justice, nonviolent alternatives to conflict, and the rights of conscience. An interfaith, tax-exempt organization, FOR promotes active nonviolence and has members from many religious, spiritual, and ethnic traditions." For more information, see http://forusa.org/about.

[34] Interview IA/PCSJA #4 05.2012

[35] In this period guerrilla groups exercised comparatively little violence against civilians; in fact, as Figure 4 shows for the municipality of Apartadó, paramilitary armies carried out most of the killings of civilians.

[36] Interview C/PCSJA #9 27.04.2014

and the early 1990s civilians perceived the presence and incursions of paramilitary as rare events. But by 1995-96 they became a regularity: "[By 1995] it was not that they [paramilitaries] were here all the time or lived among us, but they began to pass by, ask questions, and abuse the civilian population more and more often. They also began to attack guerrilla groups more often. You heard combats almost everyday."[37]

Paramilitaries progressively became the central military actor in the village and overtook control in many areas. However, not every campesino left the area or submitted to paramilitary authority and control. Initially, exhausted by high levels of violence and repression, they decided to protest in front of the government building and demand protection. Several families (around 800 campesinos) marched from San José to the city of Apartadó and established a temporary refuge in the city's coliseum.[38] After some negotiations with a government-sponsored commission, they went back home and, upon their return, some of the leaders were assassinated. In view of this response, a group of about 1,500 San José villagers opted instead for self-organization in order to find a collective, campesino-based solution to the problem. After discussing possible courses of action, the villagers sought the support of external actors, stating their determination not to leave the village while, at the same time, opting out of war.[39]

Inspired by a proposal by Monsignor Isaías Duarte Cancino, the then-Bishop of the Dioceses of Apartadó,[40] San José villagers decided to formally declare themselves neutral to the conflict and establish a Peace Community. In doing so, they pledged not to participate in any possible way in the war and disavow any form of cooperation with all armed groups, including the national army and the police. In addition, with flags,

---

[37] Interview C/PCSJA #9 27.04.2014. As the municipality-level data used in this study shows (see Figures 4 and 5 in Chapter 5), both violent activity and lethal violence against civilians significantly increased after 1995. Besides lethal violence, forced displacements also rose dramatically during these years. As village-level data collected by Valenzuela (2010) shows, 1996 and 1997 were the years that reported more cases of forced displacement in the area: in June 1996 alone, 811 people from 27 different settlements of San José left their lands.

[38] They denounced 22 extrajudicial assassinations, four forced disappearances, eight cases of torture, one indiscriminate bombing, and several cases of forced displacement. See Molano, Alfredo "La Violencia en Urabá," *El Espectador*, 05.08.2012. http://www.elespectador.com/noticias/nacional/irrespeto-neutralidad-articulo-365487.

[39] The local Catholic church (through the Dioceses of Apartadó), the Bogotá-based Inter-Church Commission for Justice and Peace (commonly referred to by its Spanish acronym, CIJP [Comisión Intereclesial de Justicia y Paz], see footnote #56 for more information), the Center for Research and Popular Education (CINEP), Pax Christi from the Netherlands, and the then-mayor of Apartadó, Gloria Cuartas, were the main initial actors discussing and supporting villagers in their decision. Although these actors were central to frame and give more definite form to the initiative according to a PCSJA leader, San José villagers already had the idea of seeking protection via a commitment to noncooperation before reaching external actors. Interview L/PCSJA#36 31.05.2014.

[40] Monsignor was later killed on the March 16, 2002 in the city of Cali, by two assassins presumably hired by the FARC. See *El Tiempo*, 2012, http://www.eltiempo.com/archivo/documento/CMS-11041045.

symbols, billboards and fences, they explicitly delineated and designated physical areas where Community members stayed, while armed groups, without distinction, could not enter or pass through. This strategic choice was as much about nonviolent resistance against violence, as it was about self-organization in specific areas to avoid displacement (at least displacement to very far away territories).

The Decision to Stay

The core of the PCSJA members' civil resistance efforts was a resolute decision to remain in their lands, and thus refuse to join the millions of internally displaced people that Colombia's civil war has generated. Although organized mass resettlement can be a strategy of noncooperation with armed groups seeking territorial and population control, in the case of the Peace Community, avoiding displacement was at the core of villagers' resistance. The region in which San José is located was targeted for strategic displacement, as the arriving paramilitaries aimed at large to get rid of disloyal communities, a strategic practice that is common in civil war (Anderson and Wallace 2012, 141; Kalyvas 2006, 222; Steele 2009; Steele 2011). In some hamlets, they gave people explicit orders to leave and issued specific ultimatums for people to vacate the land or else they will be killed.

As residents from these hamlets recall,[41] paramilitaries told them: "You have five days. If in five days we find a kid, an old man, an old woman, no matter who they are or what are they called, we do not care. We come to cut heads off."[42] And qualitative evidence reveals that this was not only a threat. Paramilitaries were serious about their intentions: "Even before the ultimatum of five days that they issued came to an end" a leader from the same hamlet recalls, "they came and started to kill people only after three days."[43] In the words of several interviewees, the situation was indeed of "either leaving or dying." Under these circumstances, for San José villagers, civil resistance constituted first and foremost a "commitment to the right of any Colombian not to be expelled from his or her land, nor attacked for staying on it" (Anderson and Wallace 2012, 142).

To be sure, many San José residents left the village during the first half of the

---

[41] To guarantee the security of villagers, I do not provide explicit names for these hamlets.
[42] Ibid.
[43] Interview L/PCSJA#8 26.04.2014

1990s.[44] Under conditions of fear, uncertainty and danger, exit seemed like a sensible option. In most contemporary war-torn countries, migration has been one of the most common ways in which people cope with violence and its effects (Lubkemann 2008). Interviews with both people who stayed and people who left suggest that most of those who had somewhere to go or the economic means to move further away left the village. Meanwhile those who stayed did so because they did not have the means to leave. As one leader of the PCSJA put it: "As people started to leave, it was only us left […] we were poor peasants, we were not people who had enough money to say 'we will leave to other places', no!"[45]

However, leaving incurs both tangible and intangible costs. It requires civilians to uproot their lives and leave behind material and nonmaterial belongings. As in many other rural areas in the country and the world, a large proportion of rural peasants depend solely on land for their subsistence (see, e.g., Scott 1976). For many of the San José residents who stayed, trying their luck elsewhere was not an option. "Nooo! And where are we supposed to go? Here we have our food. Nooo! If we leave we die out of hunger!"[46] one interviewee exclaimed when asked about the option of going somewhere else. Moreover, among those who stayed in San José, a large number had experienced forced displacement before and were not willing to assume again the costs of leaving everything behind and starting all over again. An elderly founding member of the community was clear in this regard: "Of course one did not think about leaving once again and losing everything. I have had two other displacements before in this war and I am still here, alive and kicking [laughs]."[47]

All in all, many San José residents had reasons to stay despite the violence that was affecting them. Although interview evidence suggests that many of the villagers who stayed did not have much of a choice, some leaders indicated that staying put when paramilitaries were overtly asking them to leave was in itself an act of resistance. "There

> "There was also the idea of not abandoning the territory. The idea was that of staying to try to build some strength, because being evicted like that, with no attempt to fight back, no! We had to fight!"

---

[44] See data on displacement for the village of Apartadó in Valenzuela (2010).
[45] Interview L/PCSJA#8 26.04.2014.
[46] Interview C/PCSJA#39 02.06.2014.
[47] Interview C/PCSJA#34 30.05.2014.

was also the idea of not abandoning the territory. The idea was that of staying to try to build some strength, because being displaced like that, with no attempt to fight back, no! We had to fight!"[48] Moreover, to minimize the likelihood of getting killed for staying, the decision to stay meant for many villagers that they needed to self-organize and face the situation collectively. As with the Palestinian *sumud*,[49] staying in their village, on their land, in the face of oppression in effect becomes a form of defiance (Bartkowski 2013a, 16).[50]

The Choice of Nonviolent Methods

Organizing grassroots armed resistance to counter violence is a possible course of action for communities willing to challenge and defy armed groups present in their territories (Petersen 2001). This is especially the case of communities living in the midst of a civil war, where for several reasons the opportunity to do so is more available compared to non-civil war settings (e.g., cognitive availability, availability of arms, and normalization of violence as a means). In fact, we have seen several village guards, self-defense groups and the like emerging in several civil wars (see Degregori 1999; Degregori et al. 1996; Francis 2005; Fumerton 2001; Hoffman 2007; Starn 1995). Nonetheless, San José residents opted for nonviolent methods to challenge violence. In fact, unlike other communities that have engaged in nonviolent actions in Colombia and elsewhere, violence as a method of resistance was not even contemplated as an alternative for those residing in San José. Since the beginning of the discussions and consultations on what to do, campesinos were clear about the fact that whatever they would do was going to be nonviolent. Neutrality was equated, since the very beginning, to a rejection of violence and efforts toward peacebuilding at the local level. Where did this commitment to nonviolent action come from?

There seem to be good reasons to think that the PCSJA's choice for nonviolent methods was principled and stemmed, to a large degree, from the religious profile of their initial support network and the role that the local church played during the first stages

---

[48] Interview L/PCSJA#8 26.04.2014

[49] *Sumud* is literally translated as "steadfastness." In the Palestinian interpretation, it means strong determination to stay in the country and on the land. It is likely that it has been part of the Palestinian consciousness of struggling for their land since, at least, the British Mandate.

[50] Also see Kestler-D'Amours, Jillian "In the Jordan Valley, Existence is Resistance." *Al Jazeera*, July 29, 2011.

of mounting resistance.[51] From several interviews it becomes clear, for example, that Eduard Lancheros, a human rights defender from a religious organization called Justicia y Paz, who became perhaps the most important person supporting the Community since the beginning, played a central role in the Community's choice for nonviolent action. When asked about the Community's choice for nonviolent methods, an elderly woman from the PCSJA firmly said without any probing: "Always, in each meeting, he [Eduard Lancheros] told us 'whatever happens, whatever armed groups do to you guys, you will not wield a weapon, not even a needle, you will not wield it!'"[52]

However, the evidence I have collected shows that strategic considerations were probably the most decisive in the villagers' choice for nonviolent resistance, particularly after the decision to stay neutral was made. Well aware of how asymmetric an armed struggled against heavily armed groups would be, San José residents considered that a resolute rejection of violence was almost a precondition to credibly signal armed groups their intention of staying out of war and remaining neutral. Nonviolent action was actually seen, as PCSJA's leaders put it during a group interview, as "[...] the only way to tell the paramilitaries, guerrillas, state forces and police that we didn't want them...the only way to tell them 'leave us alone, do not make us part of this war. What we want is to work, what we want is to live.'"[53]

Furthermore, by 1997, it seems that one central lesson villagers took from the recurring atrocities was that violence was not an effective means to solve disputes, because it most likely results in more violence. One founding member of the Community, who had been escaping violence for several months before creating the PCSJA, was quite clear about it: "Violence generates more violence. For example, if a young kid learns that his mom or dad was killed and decides to join the guerrillas, he will seek for vengeance for his family. So, what is he doing there? Generating more violence!"[54] Finally, interview data also show that villagers were aware of the fact that joining any of the groups in the area, or mounting any type of violent resistance, would have only accelerated the process of getting killed: "If one decides to go with the military, the guerrillas kill you. If one goes instead with the guerrillas, the paramilitaries or the army

---

[51] Interviews with external actors who worked with and supported the community in its formation told me that they recall concrete ways in which the Church tried to "evangelize" the Community and enforce certain rules of behavior, for example not drinking alcohol. Interviews #37 13.06.2015 and #47 16.07.2015

[52] Interview #39 02.06.2014

[53] Interview L(G)/PCSJA#7 25.04.2014

[54] Interview L/PCSJA#11 27.04.2014

soldiers kill you. There was nothing to do there. So I said 'the best is to be a worker, a peasant, so that if one gets killed, one gets killed while working."[55]

To be sure, these considerations were accompanied and probably enhanced by principled and moral reasons for nonviolent action endorsed by their support network, which included religious institutions. However, it is important to note that when this support network started to take shape, villagers were already committed to nonviolent methods. Moreover, this commitment to nonviolent organizing was what, in part, called the attention of many national and international organizations that began supporting the Community, as the principle resonated with them. In fact, the campesinos would eventually request a permanent presence of national and international institutions in their territory to enable their nonviolent resistance.

Guiding Principles and Organizational Structure

Following a difficult and risky drafting process, PCSJA members publicly signed and presented the PCSJA Declaration on March 23, 1997, in San José center. Campesinos, international representatives and members of national NGOs, the local church, and the local government were all in attendance. The residents took this action so as to publicly state their commitment to neutrality and noncooperation, and inform all those who were to be part of the Community as well as third parties (mainly armed groups operating in the area and the national government) about their choice and its implications.

The declaration was the outcome of an extensive process of consultation and reflected the majority will of San José residents. With the support of external actors, mainly human rights defender Eduard Lancheros and the Jesuit priest Javier Giraldo (both from the CIJP),[56] Community leaders discussed and agreed on a list of basic principles, norms of behavior and organizational structure that were to govern villagers' daily lives. External supporters and community leaders took the lead in the discussion.

---

[55] Interview C/PCSJA#14 30.04.2014
[56] According to PBI's website, CIJP is "a Human Rights NGO made up of 50 members with Catholic, Presbyterian and humanist backgrounds. The Commission accompanies communities and organizations that affirm their rights, without resorting to violence, in areas of armed conflict." For more information, see http://www.pbi-colombia.org/los-proyectos/pbi-colombia/sobre-pbi-colombia/organizaciones-acompanadas/comision-intereclesial-de-justicia-y-paz/?L=1

Regarding the interaction between external actors, community leaders and residents of the village, one peasant stated:

> They had private meetings; they, with the accompaniers, held their own meetings and coordinated other meetings for the rest of the residents. What they discussed in private was then shared with the rest of the residents who were there. It was they who understood what was and was not going on, how things were unfolding. They knew things were going to get worse. So, when they were done with their meetings, they gathered us together and informed us of the situation.[57]

However, especially in the ratification stage, everyone was welcome to participate and everyone's opinions were heard and taken into account. As Pardo (2008, 113) states, even today, more than 15 years later, members of the Community remember the process of drafting and signing the declaration as a "unifying force for the collective."

Box 1. What is the PCSJA Declaration?

The Declaration, following a standard model, consisted of two parts: the first part elaborates on the conditions that pushed campesinos of San José to create the PCSJA. The second section presents the principles, code of conduct, internal structure and formal procedures of the Community. Since the Declaration was signed, this code of conduct has regulated the behavior of its members, and an elected Internal Council carries out administrative and disciplinary/policing functions. The Declaration, among many other documents, memoires and news about the Community is available on its website (http://www.cdpsanjose.org).

---

[57] Interview P/PCSJA#43 05.06.14

Chapter 3: The Creation of the PCSJA

This process of consultation was certainly not an easy task. It was a risky enterprise to meet and discuss such a strategy in the middle of war and in the presence of several armed groups. In fact, several meetings had to be organized clandestinely or held in places civilians expected armed groups to respect, such as the church or the town's health center.[58] Leaders and rank-and-file members recall how hard it was at times to meet in the presence of the national army in San José center and paramilitaries that came along occasionally. One leader described the situation as follows:

> We had our meeting in the health center and we had to fight against the state forces because they wanted to enter and listen to what we were discussing. But no! This was for peasants and that was it! They used to say that they were the authority and that there was no neutral community or anything like that. They did not allow any private meetings, nothing clandestine.[59]

In a similar vein, a peasant who participated in several meetings recalls, "Of course we had to hold our meeting [...] in secret because the entire [village] was invaded by the army and the paramilitaries."[60]

Eventually, deliberative meetings and discussions produced the Declaration (see Box 1). In terms of self-organization, a central component of civil resistance, the PCSJA has organized several working groups and committees (in addition to the Internal Council).[61] Working groups are in charge of the collective and communal production of foodstuffs and other staple goods to ensure that basic needs are met. Committees collectively organize daily activities and projects in specific areas such as health, education, work, sports, gender and culture, among others. This functioning structure has allowed the PCSJA to survive over time, honed villagers' skills in daily self-management, and made it possible for its members to live by the principles of communal trust and solidarity.

---

[58] For the idea of "sanctuary" in the midst of war, see Mitchell (2007).
[59] Interview L/PCSJA#36 31.05.2014
[60] Interview P/PCSJA#34 30.05.2014
[61] The Declaration, principles and internal regulation are available in Spanish on the official PCSJA website: http://www.cdpsanjose.org/ As for the Internal Council, according to a 2014 War Resisters International report: "The Community elects the Internal Council once a year at one of the bi-annual assemblies of the entire populace. They meet weekly, and discuss the current situation, problems facing the Community internally and externally, and strategic direction. They also serve as the management for the communally held land and resources, unless a task [...] has been specifically delegated. The Internal Council members are the public face of the Community, and face a high personal risk." See http://www.wri-irg.org/node/23326.

As with any authentic grassroots movement, following Article 5 of the Declaration, the decision of whether or not to join the Community is individual and free. As stated in Article 2, only civilian campesinos may join the PCSJA, and they must do so on a voluntarily basis. Men and women ages 12 and above may join and leave as they please. Aspiring members must take part in informational workshops and go through a "trial period." In these workshops, prospective members learn about the history and *raison d'être* of the Community. In addition, they are introduced to the rules and expectations that govern life within the Community. Workshop leaders also present basic aspects of everyday community life, as every member is required to do community work at least once a week. Once they have attended these workshops, prospective members go through a trial period (up to three months), during which the PCSJA allows them to live as if they were full members to see if they like community life and feel comfortable complying with all the rules.

> As my dad lives here [in the Community], I came to visit. I stayed only for a few days, but one year [later] I came back to visit and ended up staying for good. So that time they told me that if I wanted to stay I had to comply with the principles and rules the Community [...] When I learned about them, I told them 'Well, I will see if I can make it. If I can't, I will just leave because I don't want to cause you trouble.' Then, I began to work in the Community [...] and they [the founding members] started to tell me how things were here before and after violence, and also told me about my family. I felt rage; it was painful to learn that the armed actors have killed my family. [...] So I reflected about the whole thing, with rage and pain, and said 'No, I better stay inside the Community. This is the only alternative.'[62]

Members comply with the following fundamental rules of behavior established by Article 3 of the Declaration. These rules illustrate the villagers' strategic principles and nonviolent methods:

---

[62] Interview C/PCSJA#35 31.05.2014

- Not to participate, directly or indirectly, in hostilities (Par. 1) – noninvolvement
- Not to carry or own arms, ammunitions and/or explosives (Par. 1, a) – nonviolent discipline
- Not to provide logistical support to any of the armed groups (Par. 1, b) – noncooperation
- Not to turn to any of the armed groups to manage or resolve internal, personal or communal disputes (Par. 1, c) – rejection of armed actors' involvement in favor of conflict resolution at the community level
- Commit to participate in community work projects (Par. 1, d) – self-organization (sometimes known as the constructive program).[63]
- Commit to fight against injustice and impunity (Art. 3, Par. 1, e) – values/cause

In addition, although not listed in Article 3, members of the Community have committed not to sell or consume alcohol within the perimeter of the PCSJA. This rule, an example of self-restraint, reinforces nonviolent discipline.

Community rules are displayed at the entrance of Community grounds.
Photo source: Author

---

[63] Interview C/PCSJA#35 31.05.2014

Figure 3. **Peace Community of San José in National and Regional Contexts**

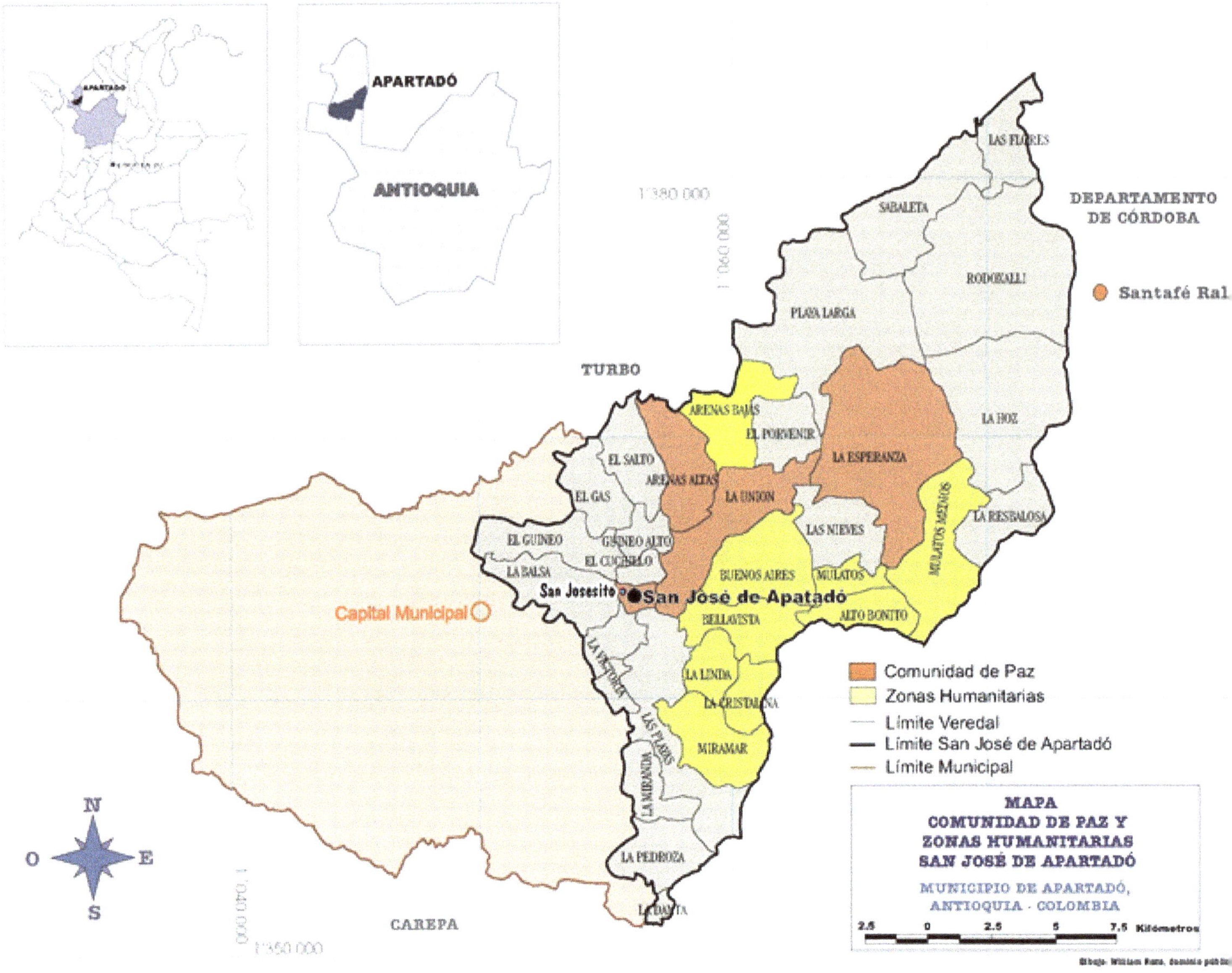

Source: cdpsanjose.org

Furthermore, Article 4 of the Declaration states the need to control the access and transit of non-members into the area where the Peace Community is settled. Following a strategy of nonviolent self-defense, the PCSJA members have gathered physically in geographically defined areas (hamlets), demarcating their residence and sphere of influence (see Figure 3). Out of the 32 hamlets that comprise San José, the PCSJA is present in at least 11 (as of 2014).[64]

In addition, in March 2005, the PCSJA established "humanitarian zones" (in yellow in Figure 3) to be used as refugee settlements to prevent further casualties and displacement during armed confrontation (CINEP 2005). Although these zones are no longer functioning as such, the logic of having refuges is a strategy to resist violence and sustain the campaign.

As mentioned previously, when the Community was founded in 1997, all members settled in San José center de Apartadó (large black dot in Figure 3). Once violence resumed, many campesinos returned to their hamlets during various "missions" organized by the Community. On February 21, 2005, eight members, including two children and a baby, were killed in the hamlets of Mulatos and La Resbalosa (east of

On February 21, 2005, eight members of the Peace Community of San José de Apartadó, including two children and a baby, were killed in the hamlets of Mulatos and La Resbalosa by militaries and paramilitaries.
Photo source: cdpsanjose.org

---

[64] These are San Josesito, Arenas, La Union, La Esperazan, Mulatos, La Resbalosa, Nain, Puerto Nuevo, Las Claras, Alto Joaquin and La Cristalina. Interview L(G)/PCSJA#7 25.04.2014.

San José center) by militaries and paramilitaries.[65] Immediately afterwards, the national government decided to open a police station in San José center. As this decision went clearly against the will of the Community and overtly violated the *raison d'être* of neutrality, PCSJA members relocated to the hamlet of La Holandita, a farmland nearby. Today it is referred to as San Josesito (small black dot in Figure 3). As we have seen in other instances of civil resistance, for example in the *hijrah* (exodus) experiences in the Middle East (Sharp 1973), for the PCSJA, relocation has been a strategic nonviolent action through which the battlefield was rearranged to avoid both displacement and compromising neutrality. Today, almost 10 years after the relocation, most of the members, including all but one of the actual members of the Internal Council[66] (as of June 2014), live in La Holandita and La Union (east of San José center).

Armed Groups' Reaction and PCSJA Response

In their analysis of the PCSJA, Anderson and Wallace (2012, 138) state that "It was [...] clear from the beginning that the armed actors in the region were not happy with San José's peace strategy." If we recall the instrumental value civilians have for armed groups waging war (Kalyvas 2006; Wickham-Crowley 1992), this should not come as a surprise. As Mohandas Gandhi rightly pointed out, "Even the most powerful cannot rule without the cooperation of the ruled."[67] For armed groups, guerrillas, paramilitaries and the armed forces alike, a self-organized community engaged in civil resistance was a threat to their interests. For one, they were blocked from accessing information necessary to advance their strategic aims. Secondly, it diminished these groups' influence on civil affairs in the village.[68] Their immediate response was accusing PCSJA members of collaborating with the enemy, followed by selective and collective targeting.[69]

As Figure 4 on page 44 shows, violence against civilians in the region was

---

[65] For detailed reconstruction of the facts, see Revista Semana's article "Por qué mataron a los niños?" http://www.semana.com/nacion/articulo/por-que-mataron-ninos/101939-3.

[66] See footnote #61 regarding the purpose and functions of the Internal Council.

[67] Cited in Bartkowski (2013a, 3).

[68] Arjona (forthcoming, chapter 3) distinguishes between a social order of surveillance, which allows for preserving territorial control but offers fewer opportunities for seizing resources, and one of "rebelocracy," which maximizes the armed group's capacity to control territory and seize resources.

[69] For the concept of collective targeting see Gutierrez Sanin and Wood 2014; Steele 2011.

noticeably high in 1997 and 1998, the two years following the Declaration. Only five days after the public declaration, armed groups launched a weeks-long armed incursion into the Community's land, killing several of its members, including important leaders. During the first nine months, according to data collected by Jesuit priest Javier Giraldo (2010; 2010), 47 members were killed in individual homicides and massacres. For the first 10 years, Amnesty International (2008) reported that at least 170 members have been killed or disappeared. By the time of the PCSJA's 15-year commemoration, Peace Brigades International (PBI) (2012) reported 210 assassinations. Moreover, PCSJA members have been victims of other forms of violence almost on a daily basis: threats, sexual abuse, burning of houses, roadblocks, blockades of foodstuffs, displacement, robbery of livestock and crop destruction, among others (Giraldo 2010).

According to several sources, the main perpetrator has been the paramilitaries, many times in alliance with the XVII Brigade of the National Army. PBI has denounced the state for its role in more than 90 percent of the cases of violence against PCSJA members (PBI 2010, n.p).[70] According to CINEP data, 130 out of 150 homicides reported from 1997 to October 2005 are attributed to the paramilitaries and the national army. This is consistent with the municipal-level data presented in Figures 4 and 5 in the next section: the state forces, the paramilitary armies, and later on the neo-paramilitaries have been responsible for the majority of civilian deaths in the municipality. What's more, they have also been responsible for most of the violent events in the first 13 years of the Community. For the majority of these crimes, investigations have not been opened and perpetrators have not been brought to justice.

In its early years, the PCSJA reacted by strengthening its support network and intensifying efforts to denounce crimes both at the national and international levels. It quickly responded to armed incursions by enlisting the support of its national networks. Yet members learned that national accompaniment was not enough to safeguard them. Thus, they (with the support of their national allies) made an extra effort to strengthen their international support networks. Today's permanent presence of FOR in the hamlet of La Union and of Operazione Colomba in the hamlet of La Holandita, as well as the

---

[70] See also Raphael Buenaventura's film *Hope for Colombia*: http://www.hopeforcolombia-film.com/#&panel1-1

center of operation PBI has in Apartadó, is the result of the Community's strategy to strengthen and internationalize its support network.

In addition to ensuring the presence of permanent international volunteers, the strengthening of international support proved useful for overcoming hardships of non-lethal violence. For example, during roadblocks, "the only vehicles that were allowed to pass unmolested were cars of Peace Brigades International and of the Diocese of Apartadó" (Anderson and Wallace 2012, 139). The Community also responded by pushing external actors to "name and shame", in their own countries, perpetrators of violence in San José. The advocacy and lobbying work by the Colombia Support Network in Madison, Wisconsin, USA and the Washington Office on Latin America in the District of Columbia, USA are two examples of this strategy.[71]

When looking at how San José villagers responded, it can be argued that armed groups' repression has backfired (Hess and Martin 2006; Martin 2006). Without any prompting, backfiring was a recurring topic in one group interview that was held with the members of the Internal Council. There, one leader stated: "The more violations against us, the stronger we become. It is in the face of these violations and attempts to exterminate us that we believe more in what we have built [...]"[72] Violence against members of the Community has in fact brought it together and strengthened ties among its members. As many interviewees highlighted, the people that the Community has lost to war are a good enough reason to continue the struggle. "We cannot start with a clean slate, because all the people we see dying in those times are part of our history. Our historical memory is of those who have fallen throughout the existence of the Community."[73]

Despite violence and impunity, the Community is still in place and firm in its determination to nonviolently resist the dynamics of war. For the last 17 years, PCSJA members have lived by the principles of noncooperation and nonviolent organizing and have been actively committed to community work.

---

[71] A more detailed discussion of the role of external actors is presented in the last part of this section as well as in Chapter 5, when discussing the "internationalized actions" of the PCSJA struggle.
[72] Interview L(G)/PCSJA#7 25.04.2014
[73] Interview P/PCSJA#11 27.04.2014

Chapter 4
The Emergence of the PCSJA: Identifying Explanatory Factors

The last section presented a detailed description of the process by which the Community was set up, delving deeper into the context in which it was created, the central choices that villagers made to give it the form it has, and the internal organizational structure. This section aims to further analyze these elements. It identifies factors that seem to be key in explaining why villagers preferred nonviolent civil resistance as a response to armed group's violence and how they act collectively. Thus, the emphasis is on factors that shape a preference for civil resistance and affect the capacity that communities have to act upon this preference. More than providing definitive answers, it proposes a set of explanatory factors that can serve to develop a theory on the emergence of civil resistance in civil war.

The Preference for Noncooperation: Violence that Stimulated Nonviolent Resistance

Armed groups increased their military activity in Apartadó in 1996 and 1997 (see Figures 4 and 5) when violence against civilians, especially by paramilitary armies, peaked. In addition, much of this activity was geared towards civilians or, at least, that more civilians were falling victim to this activity. Without implying any causal relationship, it is revealing that civil resistance in San José emerged precisely when repression peaked. The increase in violent activity shaped residents' choices and decision-making processes in many ways. "1996 was the height of paramilitary violence, in alliance with the army, in the [region] of Urabá. It was so violent that we were forced to make different choices [about how we should protect ourselves],"[74] one interviewee said.

---

[74] Interview L(G)/PCSJA#7 25.04.2014

Figure 4. **Violent Events by Perpetrator, Apartadó 1989–2010 (Including San José)**

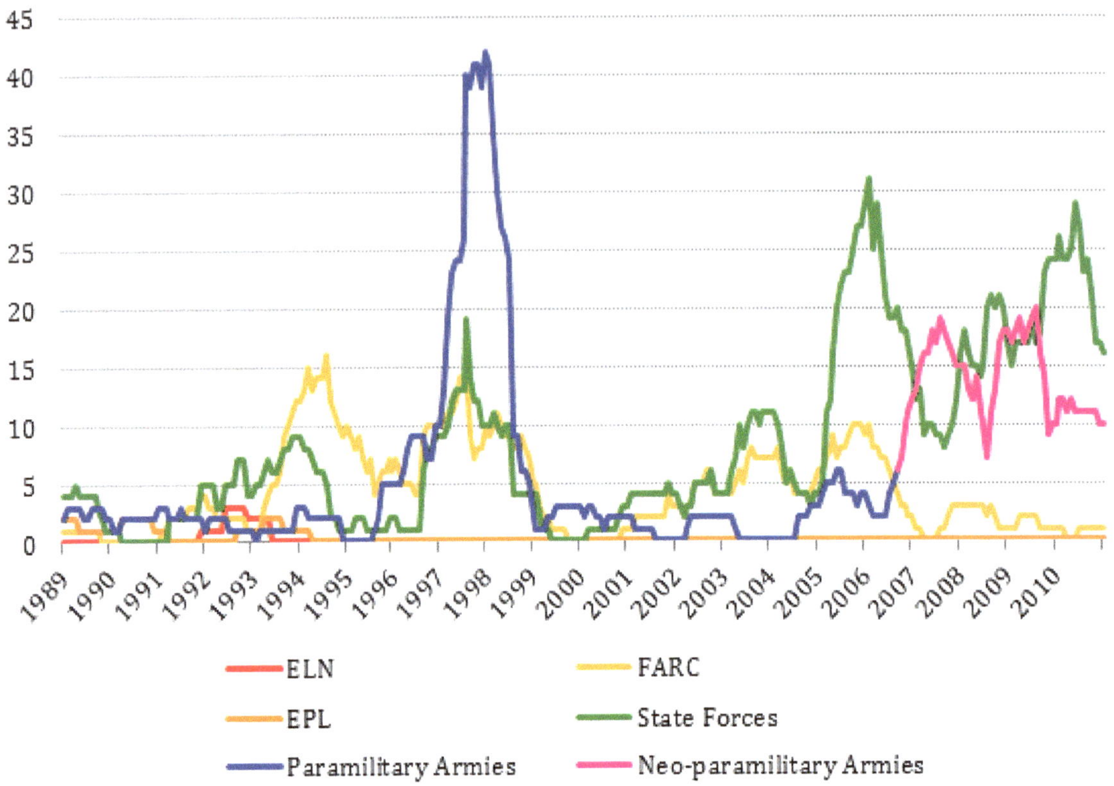

Source: Conflict Analysis Research Center (CERAC). "Colombian Armed Conflict" data set V.11.3. Data subject to revisions and updates. See Acronyms list at end of monograph for more information.

Chapter 4: The Emergence of the PCSJA: Identifying Explanatory Factors

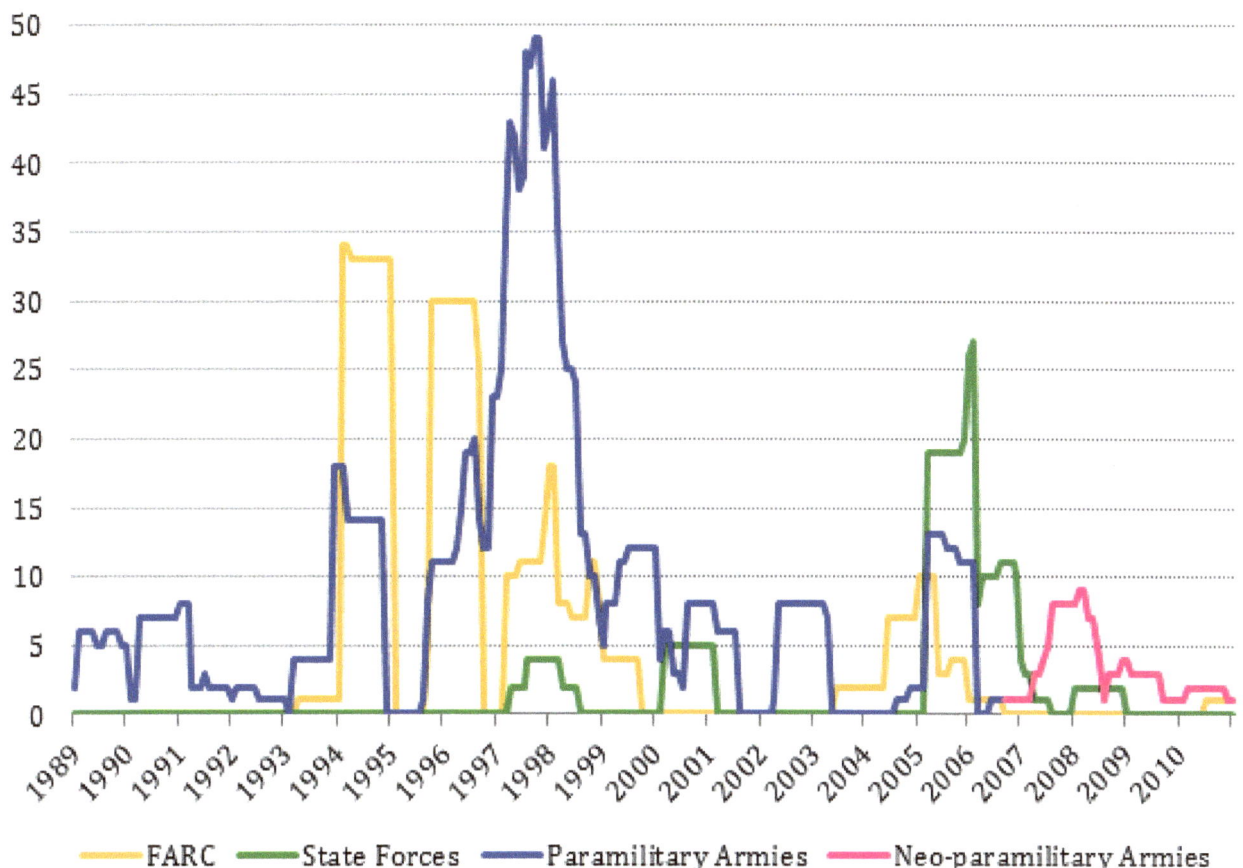

Figure 5. **Civilian Deaths by Perpetrator, Apartadó 1989 – 2010 (Including San José)**

Source: CERAC. "Colombian Armed Conflict" data set V.11.3. Data subject to revisions and updates.

However, it was not just the intensification of violence that coincided with increased presence of paramilitaries in the village that shaped villagers' preferences for nonviolent resistance. Another factor was that the violence was increasingly viewed as indiscriminate and was affecting the civilian population more directly than before. Both factors contributed to high levels of uncertainty in civilian life and left villagers with a stronger sense of vulnerability. The need to introduce more certainty into their daily lives and regain basic levels of protection pushed civilians to explore alternative courses of action. In doing so, extremely risky as it seemed, civil resistance appeared 'the only way out', at least for those who decided to stay put. As PCSJA's leaders put it in a group interview, "Through displacement we all got closer to each other [as many

initially congregated in San José center]. Seeing the way they were massacring us here, the conclusion was that there was no alternative [to self-organizing]."[75]

The paramilitary challenge to guerrilla control of San José left civilians more exposed to violence than ever. With the arrival of the paramilitary armies, civilians felt that all groups were against them and, therefore, that there was no reliable provider of protection in town. Referring to the times of guerrilla control [the 1980s and early 1990s], an elderly peasant stated: "We did not observe [guerrilla violence against civilians]. There was no violence, at least not against us, while the EPL was here; no, the FARC neither."[76] However, after the mid-1990s, with the EPL's demobilization and the arrival of the paramilitaries, things changed dramatically: "But all really went to hell when Uribe took office[77] and created the paramilitaries. Yes, with the arrival of the paramilitaries and the XVII Brigade that supported them. Then the bloodshed took place."[78]

The FARC saw the growing activities of paramilitaries and state forces as a credible threat to its own insurgent project. Under these new circumstances, the FARC seemed to have revised its strategic approach, altering the behavior it exhibited toward civilians. The FARC became more violent in its treatment of civilians from 1993 to 1999 (see Figure 5). One leader explains: "Before, the FARC was in favor of the civilian population. [When the paramilitaries arrived in the village,] the FARC became aggressive towards civilians."[79] Preserving military advantage, or even just guaranteeing their own survival, perhaps became the FARC's main concern; efforts to guarantee civilian protection seemed to have become auxiliary.

As civilians began to have more contact with the paramilitaries, they came to realize the strength of these violent groups in the area. The FARC saw the possibility of civilian defection to the enemy as more feasible and thus their need to guarantee civilian compliance became more urgent. Given that coercion has seemed for the FARC to be an instrument for forcing obedience, the guerrillas began to rely more on this tactic. As many interviewees pointed out, many innocent peasants were killed at the hands of the

---

[75] Interview L(G)/PCSJA#7 25.04.2014
[76] Interview P/PCSJA#40 03.06.2014
[77] Álvaro Uribe Vélez, president of Colombia from 2002 to 2010, was the governor of the Department of Antioquia from 1995 to 1997.
[78] Interview P/PCSJA#42 04.06.2014
[79] Interview P/PCSJA#43 05.06.2014

Chapter 4: The Emergence of the PCSJA: Identifying Explanatory Factors

FARC because of alleged collaboration with the paramilitaries and the government. At the same time, the paramilitaries were too new in town and too focused on overtaking the village to have provided protection to civilians (in the not-so-probable case they had any interest in doing so). Order, and the possibility of providing credible protection, come with control over the obedient population, (Arjona forthcoming a; Kalyvas 2006; Kasfir forthcoming), something all armed groups operating in San José lacked by 1996-97.

The way civilians perceived how this new wave of violence was affecting them further increased their feeling of under-protection. It was not an increase in violence per se, but the type of targeting armed groups were using that pushed villagers to seek alternative ways to cope with violence. With paramilitaries' challenge to the FARC's control, civilians felt that armed groups were targeting them in an indiscriminate way (either random targeting or by group association). "There [on the unpaved road leading to San José] armed groups were killing whoever they felt like killing. Kids, whatever!" one interviewee stated.[80]

This perception left civilians uncertain about the type of behaviors that could help them avoid violence. The feeling of inescapability not only pushed civilians to seek innovative courses of action, but also made them realize that, at least under the new circumstances, cooperation with any armed group would not ensure security. Indiscriminate targeting makes cooperation in exchange for protection ineffective. This is especially the case when there is no dominant actor in town, as was the case in San José in 1996-97.

Having already decided to stay, villagers began exploring alternatives. In this exercise, collective nonviolent methods became the preferred, if not the only, course of action. However, acting collectively is not an easy task and not every community with a shared preference for civil resistance has the capacity to act upon it.

---

[80] Interview P/PCSJA#14 30.04.2014

The Capacity to Resist

Evidence from Colombia shows that many villagers facing similar conditions have considered civil resistance as an option, but only a few have been able to pursue this method. Moving from the desire to resist to actual resistance is not an easy task and not every community willing to engage in civil resistance has the capacity to do so. In this regard, at least two elements are worth highlighting to understand why the PCSJA's efforts to organize were successful: prior experiences of collective action and the development of a support network with external actors.

Prior Experiences of Collective Action

Prior experiences of collective action and the active participation of many villagers in running local institutions were key in shaping San José villagers' capacity for collective action. Many members of the Community were also members of regional trade unions, campesino associations and regional/local chapters of the Unión Patriotica. These previous experiences helped villagers of San José mount their civil resistance campaign in at least three main ways. First, they exposed campesinos to collective work, which is essential for acquiring know-how and developing bonds of trust and reciprocity with others. Secondly, these experiences showed villagers that they could actually take part in shaping the institutions that govern their lives and build parallel institutions to address their own needs. Thirdly, they developed leaders who were available to engage in civil resistance, even if they were dormant for some period of time. Availability of community leaders played a significant role in the PCSJA's emergence: apart from having experience in organizing and leading campaigns, leaders themselves absorbed much of the risk associated with defying repressive actors.[81]

---

[81] Availability of leaders is a crucial factor shaping a community's capacity for collective action. Even if leaders are killed (as has happened many times in the PCSJA since its creation), it hasn't been enough to derail campaigns. The killings have weakened the PCSJA, and each time it has lost a leader it has been a tremendous shock to the Community. However, many times it has backfired by compelling surviving colleagues to take over the responsibilities of fallen ones and forge ahead.

Chapter 4: The Emergence of the PCSJA: Identifying Explanatory Factors

The Role of External Actors

The second element shaping the PCSJA's capacity for collective action was the development of a national and international network willing to support its civil resistance efforts since nearly the beginning of the process. As described earlier, San José villagers had the support of at least three external actors during the launch of their campaign: two religious-based NGOs and the local diocese. These organizations, which enjoyed higher degrees of organization and formalization, accompanied and advised campesinos in the process of exploring alternatives and giving shape to the idea of neutrality. By doing so, they contributed to the PCSJA's social organization and coordination, mainly by generating a "supportive group environment." Beyond some organizational assets, this type of environment proved to be central as it provided villagers with confidence and hope in the whole process.[82] In fact, at one point, as one of the Community leaders noted, villagers asked the CIJP[83] to provide constant accompaniment as a condition to launch the campaign and go forward with the process.[84]

The villagers counted on this organization—and in particular on Eduard Lancheros and the Jesuit priest Javier Giraldo, who had leadership skills and were regarded by campesinos as "highly knowledgeable" and "trustworthy"—to help create an encouraging environment for breaking the "law of silence" that reigns in many warzones. This inspired local residents to reveal their true preferences for nonviolent resistance in an otherwise dangerous context (Kuran 1995), and also drew more people in to get involved. Furthermore, validation of nonviolent methods by people outside of the Community reinforced residents' hope that it was a realistic choice.

Moreover, these external actors provided physical places, such as the church, that campesinos "socially appropriated"[85] for the purposes of organization and coordination. Counting on these spaces, which were safer meeting points, made an important difference in San José. As armed groups try to control and crack down on public gatherings, as we have seen in other contexts, ceremonies in these physical places

---

[82] For the concept of a "supportive group environment" see Garrison, Fireman, and Rytina 1982. See also Koloma Beck 2012, 131.
[83] See footnote #56 for a definition of this entity.
[84] Interview L/PCSJA#36 31.05.2014
[85] For this concept see McAdam, Tarrow, and Tilly 2001.

"become occasions to gather and organize in a space not fully controlled by a regime" (Bartkowski 2013b, 3).

Finally, it is important to note that this external network of support has also proven essential for the PCSJA's survival. Interviewees all agreed that the international community, in particular FOR,[86] Operazione Colomba and Peace Brigades International, have played a definitive, positive role in the Community's emergence and endurance.

---

[86] See footnote #33 for a definition of this entity's functions.

Chapter 5
Civil Resistance: The Methods of Nonviolent Action

During 17 years of nonviolent struggle, the PCSJA has adopted and employed a mixture of nonviolent methods to advance and sustain its civil resistance effort. Apart from defining guidelines for its broader resistance campaign, these methods have also defined a concrete plan of action. As in several societies across the world, this repertoire of nonviolent actions has helped San José residents to survive the burdens of war, strengthen their social and cultural fabric, build economic and political institutions, and shape identities despite extreme repression. In this section I survey the organized, purposeful and defiant nonviolent actions on which San José villagers have relied to wage their struggle.

In this subsection, I first present three broad types of nonviolent action the PCSJA has used: disruptive, contained and routinized. Then I outline how San José villagers have internationalized their struggle by working in coordination with several international organizations.

Disruptive Actions

The most overtly disruptive action used in the history of the PCSJA has been that of public demonstration. A notable example is the demonstration launched on March 23, 1997 during which villagers declared themselves the PCSJA. This act was disruptive because it was "one of the first public demonstrations of nonviolent resistance in a country where traditionally only violent means are used to solve conflicts," as noted by the co-founder and program director of the Colombia Support Network (CSN), a US-based grassroots organization working to improve the human rights situation in Colombia which has accompanied the Community since 1997 (Zarate-Laun 2012, 17).

In the presence of the Catholic church, national NGOs, members of the Parliament of the Netherlands, and some members of the local government, San José residents delivered a clear and strong message to all armed groups involved in the war: "We are no longer playing this game of perpetual killing; we are not going to help any armed group, and none of these groups will have presence in the demarcated area of our Peace Community. *Guerrillos, paras, milicos* all the same."[87]

> "We are no longer playing this game of perpetual killing; we are not going to help any armed group, and none of these groups will have presence in our Peace Community. Guerrillos, paras, milicos all the same."

This demonstration signaled the villagers' new collective identity as a nonviolent actor in the conflict; it provided clear-cut evidence of its determination to remain out of the war; and it conditioned the routine activities and behaviors of the armed groups operating in the area. Since this demonstration, warring parties have had to deal with members of the Community knowing that they would not be welcome in certain territories and not be able to obtain any form of cooperation. The capacity of armed groups to control a locality of high strategic value was drastically compromised as a result.

The public declaration was equally disruptive for the national government. On the one hand, PCSJA members conferred the exact same status to the state's armed forces as it did to illegal armed groups, the paramilitary armies and the guerrilla groups. This was a formidable challenge. At the creation of the PCSJA the then-governor of Antioquia, Álvaro Uribe Vélez (later president of Colombia for two consecutive periods [2002-10]), had the project of establishing "neutral zones" through non-cooperation with illegal armed groups, but cooperation with state forces. By contrast, the establishment of the PCSJA represented a social pact between self-organized local residents that implied carrying out several state-like activities and building institutions (see Figure 6 for concrete examples), from which the state was left out. The following statement by Uribe Vélez in

---

[87] Interview IA/PCSJA#11 05.2012

Guerrillos, paras, milicos are, respectively, colloquial forms to refer to members of the guerrilla groups, paramilitary armies, and national army.

2005, as the president of Colombia, is evidence of how concerned the government was about civilian non-compliance with the government's military objectives.

> Peace communities have the right to exist in Colombia thanks to the rights accorded by our political system. But they cannot, as is practiced in the Peace Community of San José de Apartadó, obstruct justice, reject the armed forces, prohibit the sale of licit items, or restrict the freedom of the citizens that reside there. In this Community of San José de Apartadó there are good people, but some of their leaders, sponsors and defenders are being gravely accused by residents of being auxiliaries of the FARC and of utilizing the Community to protect this terrorist organization.[88]

Apart from the public inauguration, the PCSJA has used demonstrations on several other occasions. Initially every three months, and later on every year, the PCSJA has organized a public demonstration to celebrate its existence as a Peace Community. These demonstrations also publicly reinforce its commitment to nonviolent resistance and internal solidarity. Apart from these anniversary demonstrations, the PCSJA has launched at least two large public demonstration campaigns: In 2005 PCSJA members carried out public protests, signed petitions and organized public meetings to urge the government not to build a police outpost in San José center, as doing so violated internal regulations and undermined physical security by making the area a potential military target.[89] Then, from October 31 to November 9, 2010, around 70 PCSJA members, with about 60 national and international peace workers and human rights defenders, marched through the streets of Bogotá in a display of communal identity, resilience and international solidarity. This public demonstration, called the Grace Pilgrimage, was the first time the Community was visible to Bogotá residents: "To the huts of the poorest, to the avenues of the rich and in the palaces of the government, they brought the message: 'Peace and community is possible. End violence! Support models for a new Colombia'" (Bossert 2010, n.p).[90]

---

[88] Statement by President Álvaro Uribe Vélez on March 20, 2005 during a Security Council held in the XXVII Brigade of the Army in the municipality of Carepa. Available on www.pbi-colombia.org.
[89] The decision to install this police post also went against the 1997 Inter-American Court of Human Rights ruling, which recognized that the presence of armed forces in the town inherently posed a threat of retaliatory attacks on civilians from other armed groups (Anderson and Wallace 2012, 138).
[90] A one-hour documentary following step-by-step this "pilgrimage" is available online: http://www.hopeforcolombia-film.com/.

Contained Actions

Contained actions include signing petitions, addressing letters to government officials, denouncing violence, collecting testimonies, reporting abuses, and offering declarations on a wide range of human rights abuses and crimes. These actions have been a central part of the PCSJA's resistance repertoire. It has been effective at calling the attention of the international community, including the Organization of American States and the United Nations, to the many crimes that PCSJA members have experienced and to nonviolent resistance actions they have advanced despite such violations (Giraldo 2010; Zarate-Laun 2012, 16). These actions have given the PCSJA national and international recognition and legitimacy.

PCSJA members reproduced the memorial of members' names in a mural on the Community school.
Photo courtesy of Amnesty International Mexico.

The central role of violence and armed groups' *de facto* control in the context of the PCSJA struggle has rendered the use of contained actions particularly contentious and defiant. Moreover, tactics that we have observed in other contexts, such as collecting testimonies and offering public declarations, have taken highly innovative forms in the PCSJA case. For example, each time a member of the Community was killed, villagers inscribed the member's name onto a stone that they picked from the river and painted in a different color. Villagers shared testimonies with external actors so the latter could relay and denounce the abuses to larger international audiences.[91] This is the case, for instance, of the 2006 Colombo-Swiss documentary Until the Last Stone (the original title in Spanish is Hasta la última piedra) by Juan José Lozano, a prominent Colombian filmmaker who has travelled the world providing evidence of the widespread human rights abuses to which the Peace Community has fallen victim.

---

[91] Unfortunately the memorial does not exist anymore. When the PCSJA relocated from San José to La Holandita they had to leave the memorial behind. The military destroyed the memorial in an attempt to erase any trace of the PCSJA. In La Holandita, however, several PCSJA members reproduced the memorial on a mural in a wall of the Community's school (see photo).

Chapter 5: Civil Resistance: The Methods of Nonviolent Action

Routinized Actions

San José villagers' daily lives are governed by a set of routines. Committee and working group activities, training workshops, Internal Council meetings and "community days" have all consistently reinforced the Peace Community's identity and meaning. These activities have also helped solve many challenges inherent to self-organization and institution building—both of which have been central to the PCSJA's nonviolent resistance. As one interviewee put it: "We all agreed on the need to self-manage everything in the Community. Restaurants, schools... everything. Whatever you see functioning here is not managed by or with the government. Everything is managed by us."[92]

The different committees and working groups have served as platforms for Community members to carry out certain tasks and to develop grassroots, independent institutions in areas such as education, production and health. Internal Council meetings, held every Wednesday (at the moment of this research), have served as the forum for functional decision-making. Issues discussed range from accepting financial help from an external organization or taking part in an international campaign, to accepting or declining visit requests by journalists, researchers and others. The forum is also used to analyze the status quo of the conflict, assess new risks and challenges and identify community needs. These gatherings are closed to the public and sometimes can last an entire day.[93] Finally, "community days", taking place every Thursday (at the time of the manuscript's publication) serve to carry out necessary tasks such as cleaning common areas, building trails connecting hamlets, and cultivating, collecting and selecting cacao for export purposes. Above all, the "community days" bring all members together, reinforcing unity and solidarity.

Internationalized Actions: The Struggle Beyond Borders

The PCSJA has established strong and enduring alliances with several international NGOs, think tanks, advocacy groups and religion-based organizations, among others. A

---

[92] Interview C/PCSJA#13 28.04.14
[93] Depending on the issues at hand, decisions are made in consultation with every member of the Community. Taking advantage of the fact that the Internal Council gathers on Wednesdays in the same hamlet, members of the council meet with support network representatives to discuss upcoming activities and, when needed, to make formal requests for international physical accompaniment.

number of "internationalized actions" that have grown out of this support network have been key to advancing and sustaining the struggle. For the internationals, these actions can be labeled as physical and/or political accompaniment. Although intimately related, both types of actions follow different logics. Underlying physical accompaniment is the idea that having international people in the field helps to protect villagers by increasing the costs of victimization. As for political accompaniment, the idea that raising awareness about the events of San José among international audiences puts pressure on the Colombian government to respect the PCSJA's neutrality and take measures to address abuses.

The message behind international accompaniment is straightforward: "We are watching and we are reporting to the international community."[94] FOR and other organizations have set up programs of physical accompaniment on the ground. Although the concrete *modus operandi* of each organization and their protocols differ, volunteers of these organizations live in different hamlets of San José, take part in many of the daily activities and in some cases support Community projects. However, their main task is that of acting as "unarmed bodyguards" (Mahony 1997): regularly accompanying Community members, mostly leaders, when they must move from one hamlet to another or visit nearby areas.[95]

In turn, political accompaniment follows instead the logic of "When the government in Colombia does not want to listen and act, we have to try with our own governments and with the international institutions based in our countries. Maybe they will make them listen and act."[96] Therefore, most of the actions carried out by internationals involved in political accompaniment is taken beyond Colombian borders, but always with the aim of bringing back pressure, in a "boomerang effect" (Keck and Sikkink 1998; Keck and Sikkink 1999), on the Colombian government through formal appeals by recognized international parties. As put by an official working for the Colombia chapter of the Washington Office on Latin America (WOLA): "Political support or accompaniment is about doing our best to influence, in our own countries, our government's policies towards Colombia in a way that will make Colombian officials recognize what is going

---

[94] Interview IA/PCSJA#1 04.2012

[95] Who needs accompaniment and when is decided in a dialogue between the Internal Council and the representatives of the accompanying organizations, which commonly takes place the same day the Internal Council meets.

[96] Interview IA/PCSJA#2 04.2012

on in the country, seek justice and fight impunity."[97]

To achieve this influence, contained actions, such as addressing letters and petitions to high officials of foreign countries with strong leverage on Colombian politics, have been a common strategy. A concrete example is a letter signed by over 25 international NGOs in March 2005 addressed to then-US Secretary of State, Condoleezza Rice, following the February 2005 killing of eight Community members.

> *Most of the action carried out by international actors involved in political accompaniment is taken beyond Colombian borders, but always with the aim of bringing back pressure, in a "boomerang effect" on the Colombian government through formal appeals by recognized international parties.*

> In light of allegations of involvement by members of the Colombian military, it is essential that the US government sends a strong signal by insisting that an effective investigation be conducted by civilian authorities. The State Department must include this case in its evaluation of Colombian compliance with US human rights conditions, and must refrain from certification until a credible investigation has been completed.[98]

Internationalized actions not only aim to shape responses by the Colombian government, but also to influence US foreign policy towards Colombia. As expressed by a Colombia expert working for WOLA, much of what US-based organizations do is aim to shift US foreign policy towards respect for human rights, socio-economic justice, conflict resolution through peaceful means, and strengthening of civil society.[99] This is not to say, however, that political accompaniment is limited to the United States. The Community's efforts have also targeted international entities. Among the robust examples of action at the level of international entities include: The Inter-American Commission on Human Rights' formal requests for provisional measures to ensure adequate protection to Community members, later endorsed by the Colombian Constitutional Court in three

---

[97] Interview IA/PCSJA#3 05.2012.
[98] Final draft Letter to Honorable Condoleezza Rice provided by WOLA to the author.
[99] Interview IA/PCSJA#3 05.2012

different decisions (in 2003, 2004 and 2007); and the creation of a Special Commission in 2000 to investigate abuses against the PCSJA, with the participation of the UN High Commissioner for Human Rights.[100] In Europe, organizations such as Tamera in Portugal, Operazione Colombia in Italy and Amnesty International in London have also advocated on behalf of the PCSJA in their home countries and before EU bodies. They have done so both through conventional means (such as writing letters to EU parliamentarians and other high officials), and less conventional tactics (such as screening films, sponsoring demonstrations and bringing PSCJA leaders to testify before EU audiences). For example, Tamera played an important role in organizing the Grace Pilgrimage to Bogotá in 2010, and in producing the film Hope for Colombia. PBI, among others, was instrumental in organizing a European tour in November 2012, during which two Community leaders visited several European cities to raise awareness and gain support for their cause. While in London, they had the unique opportunity to meet with officials from the Foreign and Commonwealth Office, several MPs in Westminster, the Law Society, and the All-Party Parliamentary Group for International Corporate Responsibility and for Human Rights.

Tactics of the PCSJA's Nonviolent Struggle

The vast array of nonviolent tactics used by the PCSJA constitutes a powerful instrument for community organizing and resistance. This impressive tactical diversity has laid the foundation for the emergence of the Community and, to this day, helps sustain its resilience.

Earlier in this monograph, a basic categorization of methods was presented: disruptive, contained and routinized. However, a more elaborate categorization would be instrumental in further exploring this array of tactics. This section draws on Gene Sharp's (Sharp 1973) comprehensive list of nonviolent actions to break down and systematize the wide spectrum of methods used by the PCSJA in spite of repressive conditions.

Figure 6 presents a basic map of the tactics, by category, as they appear (with more detail) in Figure 7. Refer to each of the tactics in Figure 6 to navigate to a detailed description of the actions included in Figure 7. The categories informed by Sharp's

---

[100] See petition letter sent by Javier Giraldo S.J. to President Juan Manuel Santos on November 3, 2010: http://colombiasupport.net/ Accessed April 2012.

scholarship are: 1) methods of nonviolent protest and persuasion; 2) methods of social noncooperation; 3) methods of economic noncooperation;[101] 4) methods of political noncooperation; 5) methods of nonviolent intervention.

Figure 6. **Nonviolent Tactics Used by PCSJA by Category**

Protest and persuasian	Noncooperation		Nonviolent intervention
Public declarations	Social	Political	Nonviolent occupation
Letter-writing Displayed communications Leaflets/pamphlets Display of symbols Display of portraits Singing Marches/parades Demonstrative funerals Paying homage Teach-ins	Sanctuary Protest emigration Refusal to sell Reverse strike	Withdrawal of support Boycotting elections Boycotting gov't bodies Withdrawal from public schools Boycotting gov't organizations Refusal to assist enforcement agencies	New social patterns Alternative institutions Alternative communications Alternative markets Dual sovereignty/parallel gov't

---

[101] At this stage, the research did not identify methods used by the villagers that would fall neatly into the category of economic noncooperation. However, this does not preclude the possibility.

Figure 7. **Nonviolent Actions of the PCSJA**

Gene Sharp's Methods	Concrete Examples from the PCSJA
Methods of Nonviolent Protest and Persuasian	
Formal Statements	
Public speeches / Declarations of indictment & intention / Public statements	Among several public declarations during the PCSJA's nonviolent struggle, the most important one took place on March 23, 1997 through which the Peace Community was officially declared.
Letters of opposition or support / Declarations by organizations and institutions	The PCSJA and its national and international support network have used this method repeatedly. They have sent several letters to high-level officials of the Colombian government, including the president, denouncing human rights violations and highlighting the high levels of impunity that are explicit in these violations. A notable example is the June 17, 2004 letter to President Alvaro Uribe Velez (cc. Colombia's vice-president, Francisco Santos; Colombia's Minister of Foreign Affairs, Carolina Barco; Director of the South America Division of Foreign Affairs Canada, José Herran-Lima; and the Assistant Secretary for the Bureau of Democracy – Human Rights and Labor of the US Dept. of State, Lorne Craner) and signed by over 40 representatives of US and Canada-based religious, human rights, and civil society organizations. In this letter the representatives affirmed their support for the US-based organizations that accompany the PCSJA and expressed their concern regarding the president's statements questioning the legitimacy of international human rights organizations' work vis a vis the PCSJA. See here: http://forusa.org/programs/colombia/col-pp-update-0704B.html.
Communications with a Wider Audience	
Banners, posters and displayed communications	In every hamlet where the PCSJA is present, villagers have displayed banners and clipboards to delineate their territory and inform third parties about their principles and behavioral norms. PCSJA also communicates with a wider audience via their own website (http://cdpsanjose.org/) and that of their domestic and international partners.

Chapter 5: Civil Resistance: The Methods of Nonviolent Action

Leaflets, pamphlets and books (literature and speeches advocating resistance)	PCSJA has regularly used leaflets and pamphlets to communicate to a wider audience, promote its projects and denounce crimes. For example, actors in PCSJA's support network have released PCSJA-endorsed books and videos. These means of diffusion resemble what Gene Sharp calls a strategy of "rejection of authority" via "literature advocating resistance." Illustrative examples include: - The edited volume *Sembrando Vida y Dignidad* by the Italian Solidarity Network, Colombia Vive, published in Italian and Spanish in 2009, celebrating the 10th anniversary of the Peace Community as a special issue of the journal *Quaderni Satyagraha*. - The book Fusil o Toga. Toga y Fusil published in 2010, by Jesuit priest Javier Giraldo reporting and denouncing human rights violations against PCSJA. - The 2006 film *Hasta la Última Piedra* by Juan Lozano narrating the relocation of PCSJA to La Holandita as a response to the government's decision to set up a police station in downtown San José.
Symbolic Public Acts	
Display of flags and symbols	The PCSJA displays flags, banners and clipboards with their symbol at various strategic points throughout their territory.
Display of portraits	The PCSJA displays portraits of members who have been killed in marches and other public acts. These portraits are also displayed in the main kiosk of La Holandita. Some of these portraits are available in CINEP's publication, "San Josesito de Apartadó, la otra versión" (Spanish only) See here: http://www.nocheynicbla.org/node/50.
Music	
Singing	The PCSJA has its own anthem written by Aníbal Jiménez, former member of the Internal Council murdered in the massacre of April 4, 1999. Other songs tell the story of how the PCSJA came to be and give a sense of how residents have suffered. The text and audio of the anthem are available online: http://cdpsanjose.org/?q=/node/11.
Processions	
Marches / parades	The PCSJA has organized and taken part in several marches and parades. This practice predates — and is considered one of the precursors to — the creation of the PCSJA: in 1996, several area residents marched from downtown San José to Apartadó, occupying the latter's coliseum for several days in protest against violence. A commission was later created to investigate the various violent events denounced by the protesters. Several leaders of the march were killed upon their return to the village.

	Honoring the Dead
Demonstrative funerals	The PCSJA celebrated their 17th anniversary on March 23, 2014, which they consider one of the "most emblematic moments" of their struggle. During this event they honored the dead in an act that falls under what Sharp calls "demonstrative funerals": Several PCSJA members marched to and through Apartadó carrying a five-meter long coffin with the names of more than 260 people they have lost to war. The march concluded just outside the general prosecutor's building, where the coffin was left with flowers and messages. By doing so, they honored the dead, saying "No more death, no more torture" and re-stating their stand against impunity. Pictures and a short video of this event are available online: http://cdpsanjose.org/?q=node/311 and http://www.youtube.com/watch?v=_CSW1D4eHws.
Homage at burial places	To pay homage to the dead, the PCSJA built its own symbolic "burial place." The memorial is made of stones from the river, which members painted in different colors and marked with names of those who were killed. At one point, the symbolic "burial place" had over 150 stones. As with many other PCSJA symbols, the military destroyed the memorial when villagers had to relocate to La Holandita, leaving the memorial behind. As it was too difficult to build the memorial again from scratch, it now appears in mural form on a wall in La Holandita. The film *Hasta la Última Piedra* (Until the Last Stone) is named after this memorial. The memorial is shown several times in the film, available online at http://protectionline.org/es/2013/08/08/hasta-la-ultima-piedra-documental-de-juan-jose-lozano-sobre-la-comunidad-de-san-jose-de-apartado/.
	Public Assemblies
Teach-ins / assemblies of protest and resistance	In the formative years, teach-ins (often clandestine) were held. Community leaders (and later on, external actors) spoke about the situation in the area, and several campesinos expressed their different viewpoints and explored alternatives to cope with war in their village. Interviewees recall these "teach-ins" as central to the emergence of the PCSJA, as they contributed to overall resolve to act and the greater understanding of what it takes to remain neutral. Many interviewees recall as influential and edifying the role of Eduard Lancheros, an external organizer and speaker coming from a Bogotá-based religious NGO.[102] Larger teach-ins, involving members of other resisting communities in the country, have also taken place as part of the university. This university was borne out of the Network of Resisting Communities, a group of Colombian campesinos, indigenous and afro resisting communities. The first teach-in took place in August 2004 in Arenas Altas, one of the PCSJA's hamlets. The university is described by one of PCSJA's leaders as "a place for theoretical and practical discussion. The idea is to share knowledge and experiences between the University and each of the communities" (Interview L/PCSJA#36 31.05.2014).

[102] Despite not being a campesino himself, Eduard later became a full member of the PCSJA and spent most of his days in the village. Eduard was widely considered as one of the process' main leaders and sources of inspiration. His body is buried in La Holandita.

Chapter 5: Civil Resistance: The Methods of Nonviolent Action

	Methods of Social Noncooperation
	Withdrawal from the Social System
Sanctuary	Sanctuary was a central strategy in the formative years of the PCSJA during which meetings and discussions were held in secret as opponents controlled and violently repressed public gatherings. Campesinos often used the local church and health center of downtown San José to hold these meetings. As one leader noted, "They [armed groups, mainly the military] were always there. We had to hide. So it was better to have our conversations in the health center or in other places where armed groups were not going to look for us or were not going to attack that easily" (Interview L/PCSJA#48 05.2012). Moreover, campesinos of the region have occasionally withdrawn to places where the likelihood of armed groups attacking them is lower and then return to their hamlets when violence resumed. This practice has not been limited to Community members, as the PCSJA has also created sanctuaries (such as the no longer functioning humanitarian zones) to which even non-member residents of the area could to seek protection.
Protest emigration (*hijrat*)	Although not a pure instance of *deshatyaga* or *hijrat* as "migrants" remained within the state's jurisdiction, peasants relocated to La Holandita. In doing so, the Community practiced a form of what Sharp calls "protest emigration." Resisters left downtown San José not only because the presence of a police station put them at higher risk of a guerrilla attack, but also as an expression of disapproval and protest against a state measure that clearly violated their principle of neutrality.
	Methods of Economic Noncooperation
Refusal to let or sell property	The PCSJA refuses to give or sell survival goods or property to armed groups. The small shops in La Holandita, for example, do not sell products to any actor that carries arms or to any person known to belong to an armed group, including the national army and the police. Villagers are well aware of the fact that selling goods to armed individuals (let alone land) would be a favor to them and would further enable their activities, including perpetrating violent acts. Refusing to sell goods puts armed groups in a tough spot.
Peasant / farm workers reverse strike or boycott	Although not formally on strike, campesinos of the PCSJA refuse to work as *jornaleros* (day laborers) for others, especially for those who have any sort of link with armed actors (which is often the case with large landowners) or deal with any illicit crops that feed the war, such as coca crops. Not only do campesinos refuse to work for others (a strike or boycott) with links to armed groups, instead they choose to work for themselves and the community (a reversed action that is a step further from a simple strike or boycott and includes a constructive element.)

Methods of Political Noncooperation	
Rejection of Authority	
Withholding or withdrawal of allegiance / refusal of public support	The main tenet of the PCSJA's struggle is its commitment to noncooperation. This noncooperation implies, in its most fundamental sense, withholding or withdrawing any sort of allegiance to armed groups present in the territory. This is clearly stated in the behavioral norms stipulated in the Declaration. Article 3 reads, "The members of the PCSJA refuse to provide any type of support to the parties in conflict."
Citizens' Noncooperation with Government	
Boycott of elections	Although the PCSJA does not overtly boycott elections, some of its leaders believe they should not "get mixed up with politics" and therefore refuse to participate in elections. Some even advise members not to do so as an act of refusal to recognize state legitimacy.
Boycott of government departments, agencies and other bodies	The PCSJA refuses to cooperate with all governmental offices and agencies responsible for public order and security, including the army and police. As Sharp notes, this noncooperation may sometimes be conducted at the financial expense of the noncooperators, involving refusal to accept government loans, grants-in-aid, and the like. The Community refuses to accept government money to compensate families for relatives who have been killed. In a public declaration against the "Victims' Law", [103] the PCSJA stated, "On ethical grounds, we [will separate ourselves] from those families who accept money as a compensation for the crimes that have been committed against their loved ones while tolerating impunity for those crimes." In fact, several interviewees mentioned specific cases of former members who either had to leave the Community because they accepted this money, or left it to be in a position to take the money. The declaration against the law is available online: http://www.redcolombia.org/index.php/regiones/centro/antioquia/1449-comunidad-de-paz-de-san-jose-apartadte-ley-de-victimas.html.

---

[103] The Victims' Law was signed by President Juan Manuel Santos in June 2011. The legislation aims to provide financial and other reparations to victims of human rights abuses and return deserted or stolen land to those who have been displaced internally.

Chapter 5: Civil Resistance: The Methods of Nonviolent Action

Withdrawal from government educational institutions	Resistance has gone beyond protection from overt violence to include institution building. For example, overcoming the fact that violence has driven away state-employed teachers and that the Ministry of Education refused to send new ones, the PCSJA has managed to establish their own school in La Holandita. Leaders quickly learned that they needed a different type of education to strengthen and promote the values of Community life and cooperation (Interview L(G)/PCSJA#7 25.04.2014). As one of the teachers in La Holandita said: "Education here has to be different, because it is part of the resistance process. We teach resistance and we teach peace, therefore we cannot reproduce the values of individualism and competition that the state wants to impose" (Interview E/PCSJA#10 4.27.2014). The University of Resistance/Campesino University and the Training Center "Aníbal Jiménez" are integral parts of the education system the PCSJA created after withdrawing from the state's education system.
Boycott of government-supported organizations	The PCSJA has refused to take part in several initiatives proposed by various organizations as it views them as instruments of the government. The PCSJA refused to take part in the National Center of Historical Memory's effort to document the experiences of communities that have been affected by Colombia's longstanding conflict. When asked why there is no record of the PCSJA, researchers and Center representatives explained that the Community refused to respond to informational inquiries for the report due to the Center's links with the national government (Interviews G/#29 13.05.2014 and G/#3 03.04.2014). When asked about working with the Center, a leader of the Community replied: "No, no. We didn't do it. We walk in a completely different way. For us, working with them is like legitimizing all their [government] injustices and that is not for us." (Interview L/PCSJA#36 05.31.14).
Refusal of assistance to enforcement agents	As an act of political noncooperation, the PCSJA overtly and radically refuses to provide or disclose any type of information (or any other strategic or survival asset) to the government's enforcement agents. The armed forces of the state are given exactly the same treatment the Community gives to other armed parties to the conflict, left-wing guerrilla groups and right-wing paramilitaries.
Refusal to accept appointed officials	The PCSJA has refused to accept or recognize appointed officials to operate in its area. Perhaps the most notable example was in 2005 when it refused to accept the police post in downtown San José. Its refusal went as far as moving out of the downtown area and starting anew elsewhere to avoid dealing with these officials.

Methods of Nonviolent Intervention	
Physical Intervention	
Nonviolent occupation	Due to two massacres perpetrated by armed groups in September 1996 and February 1997, most of the families living in downtown San José de Apartadó fled, leaving almost every house empty (except for three families, according to the Community's testimonies). The PCSJA is composed of people who, facing the need to leave their hamlets, decided to stay in their village by (provisionally) moving together to its urban center. This relocation can be considered an act of "nonviolent occupation" as campesinos "occupied" empty houses in downtown San José despite being explicitly ordered by armed groups to leave the village. For one of my interviewees from the hamlet of La Unión, what they did was explicitly an occupation. "When we arrived in downtown San José [from La Unión], there were no more than three families. Apart from that, houses were empty. So we arrived there and occupied those houses. Each family occupied one or two houses. We had to be very careful not to damage the doors or the things that were left there because that was not ours. We did not want the owners to find their things ruined if they were to come back" (Interview P/PSCJA#40 03.06.14).
Social Intervention	
Establishing new social patterns	This type of social intervention complements and sustains the PCSJA's baseline strategy of noncooperation. New social patterns that emerged from PCSJA's rules for daily living fit well with what Sharp refers to as "planned and organized opposition." Even new patterns of interaction that apparently are not part of "organized opposition", such as abstaining from alcohol, are in fact part of planned resistance. The idea of not drinking is twofold: minimizing the room for violent fights among members and minimizing the likelihood of unintentionally providing armed groups with information (Interview L(G)/PCSJA#7 25.04.2014).
Alternative social institutions	The creation and growth of a number of formal and informal social institutions over the last 17 years have overtly challenged pre-existing institutions. The University of Resistance/Campesino University and the school in La Holandita are clear examples in the field of education. The accompaniment schemes developed with international support are a good example in the field of security and protection provision. Organizing members into working groups is an example in the field of social and cultural activities. A working group to study the benefits of local medical plants for treating illness is an example in the field of health.
Alternative communication system	The PCSJA created a communitarian radio station called "Voces de Paz" (Voices of Peace). Although the radio station was fully prepared to go on air, it never obtained a license from the government to do so. Nevertheless, it still managed to advance several projects via the internet as a "virtual radio station." The first radio show was held in March 2007 to commemorate the 10th anniversary of the PCSJA. Available online: http://cdpsanjose.org/?q=/taxonomy/term/11. In La Holandita today, Voices of Peace uses a public broadcasting system to communicate announcements, plays the Community's anthem on "community days", and convenes people to work or hold meetings.

Economic Intervention	
Alternative markets / alternative economic institutions	The PCSJA understood early on that to sustain its resistance it needed to develop an alternative, self-sufficient economy. This was of prime importance, as armed groups established roadblocks in the main road to downtown San José and carried out economic blockades. Aside from producing what they needed to survive, the Community began exporting its products by way of Fair Trade networks. For several years it exported "banana primitive" (baby bananas) to Germany, and today it distributes organic cacao to Lush, a handmade cosmetics company headquartered in the United Kingdom and present in several countries around the world. Additionally, the Community is constantly working on production and preservation of native flora and fauna projects. Alternative markets and alternative economic solutions are among the central topics discussed when resisting communities gather at the University of Resistance/Campesino University.
Political Intervention	
Dual sovereignty and parallel government	At the local level, the PCSJA has created a parallel government. It has separated from most (if not all) governmental institutions and agencies, and has also developed its own governing institutions. This "new government" is clearly reflected in its own internal structure, with its own decision-making bodies, quasi-judiciary and conflict resolution mechanisms, rules of procedure and behavioral norms.

Chapter 6
Conclusion: Lessons from the PCSJA

This monograph presented a detailed empirical treatment of the emergence of the Peace Community of San José de Apartadó in northwestern Colombia —a civil resistance actor—and not mere victims—in the midst of civil war. It provided a comprehensive description of the process of creation, the internal and organizational structures of the PCSJA, the rules that govern members' lives, and the multiplicity of methods of nonviolent action they have used. In addition, it advanced a more theoretically informed analysis, although still preliminary, of the forces that pushed villagers to nonviolently resist against heavily armed groups and the factors that gave them the capacity to organize and act collectively.

To conclude, this section draws some lessons from the PCSJA case that could serve as general guidelines for the work of two sets of actors: international accompaniers and peacemakers. First, it highlights some elements that could be of interest for any organization willing to support, as an accompanier, similar resistance campaigns in Colombia or abroad in an effective, responsible and safe manner. Second, it identifies general implications that civil resistance experiences might have for efforts to bring a conflict to an end and rebuild society and state institutions. In particular, this section underscores several messages that the PCSJA case offers to the current Colombian peace negotiations. More research, and ideally of a comparative fashion, on the emergence, trajectories and outcomes of civil resistance in civil war settings is needed to produce a solid theoretical framework for understanding the phenomenon. Such an understanding will inform and improve governmental and nongovernmental interventions in more specific and concrete ways.

For External Actors Willing to Support Resisting Community as an Accompanier

- The support of external actors, national or international, should always be mindful not to undermine grassroots ownership and autonomy.
- External actors' decision of whether or not to accompany a community must be based on a solid analysis of specific civil war dynamics on the ground, especially the type of armed actors involved and the reasons for their actions.
- To remain neutral, external actors should be as explicit as possible, and with all parties involved in the conflict, about their presence in the area, their intentions and the role(s) they intend to play.
- For physical accompaniment to be effective in protecting civilians, the presence of volunteers on the ground must be backed by a network of organizations abroad that reinforces credibility of potential sanctions against acts of violence.

The PCSJA case reveals that there is a clear role for external actors to play in both the emergence and maintenance of a civil resistance campaign in the midst of civil war—in particular, as physical or political accompaniers. However, as one of the main PCSJA leaders stressed, local villagers should take charge of the process and external actors should remain in support roles. As it has been highlighted elsewhere (Mitchell and Hancock 2007; Hancock and Mitchell 2012) the successful functioning of peace communities (or "peace zones") requires high levels of autonomy and local ownership. External actors should always be careful not to undermine grassroots ownership and autonomy.

Furthermore, the decision to accompany a community must be based on a solid (and consistently updated) understanding of civil war dynamics and processes underway in proximity to an ongoing resistance campaign. Misinterpretations about the situation on the ground and, in particular, erroneous assessments of armed groups' incentives to

Chapter 6: Conclusion: Lessons from the PCSJA

exercise violence against civilians could lead to the escalation of violence rather than to its deterrence.[104] The baseline assumption that armed groups wish to avoid external pressure needs to be assessed against a detailed analysis of the type of armed actor at hand and of the drivers of this actor's behavior. Not every armed group is equally likely to respond to physical accompaniment with restraint; therefore, differentiated approaches are needed.[105] A good understanding of the variation of armed groups' organizational structures and behavior towards civilians should be at the foundation of any external actor's decision to support a community or not.[106]

The PCSJA case also offers other lessons about how to proceed once the decision to support has been made. To maximize the likelihood of being effective in their accompaniment, external actors should be as explicit as possible, and with all parties involved in the conflict, about their presence in the area, their intentions and the role they will be playing. This transparency is key to avoid accusations of taking sides. This is especially important for the safety and security of both organizations' staff and resisting villagers. Mistaking actors as collaborators with the enemy has been found to be one of the central drivers of armed groups' violence against non-combatants in civil war: when seen as such, they immediately become a target.[107]

Finally, it is of utmost importance for international supporting organizations to be aware that a visible and credible network of organizations and allies abroad should back physical accompaniment on the ground. This network is what raises the visibility of violent acts beyond Colombian borders and enables far-reaching lobbying and advocacy efforts. This international clout is what increases the costs to armed groups that use violence against activists.[108] As a high-ranking official of an organization that supports the PCSJA puts it, "You better watch out, we are observing here and reporting abroad."[109] If the violent actors believe that what they do will be noticed abroad and that sanctions and condemnation might follow, the likelihood that they show restraint in their actions increases.

---

[104] See Hultman 2010. Although not addressing the specific case of "unarmed bodyguards", the author examines the short-term effects of peace operations on the intensity of violence against the civilian population in internal conflicts. Her analysis demonstrates how important it is to understand the conflict dynamics to foresee the range of impacts that well-intentioned operations may have.
[105] See Masullo and Lauzurika 2014; Mampilly 2011.
[106] See Weinstein 2007; Kalyvas 2006; Arjona forthcoming a; Metelits 2010.
[107] See, among others, Kalyvas 2006.
[108] See Mahony 1997, 209
[109] Interview IA/PCSJA#1 04.2012

For Policymakers Working to Bring Peace in War-Torn Countries

- Although victimization is the most pervasive form of civilian involvement in war, civilians caught in the cross-fire are not confined to the role of passive victims; they have agency and can become agents of change.
- Recognizing and understanding civil resistance campaigns could help identify local challenges and call for specific interventions in the creation of a more stable post-peace agreement environment. Dealing with a resisting community should not be the same as dealing with a displaced community or a community that lived under the control of one armed group for many years.
- Civil resistance creates capacity in everyday life, maintains local order and produces local legitimacy, and identifies needs and how to meet those needs. These campaigns should be seen as potential opportunities rather than obstacles to the peace process.

Since November 2012, the Colombian government and the FARC have been holding formal peace talks in La Havana to end more than five decades of civil war. As the case explored in this monograph reveals, war shapes civilians' lives in substantial ways. In wartime, civilians experience different social processes—the transformation of social actors, structures, norms and practices (Wood 2008b)—that are likely to leave enduring legacies. In the perspective of designing and implementing peace policy, ignoring these processes and their legacies can lead to important drawbacks. The PCSJA case, involving processes of political mobilization, organization and redefinition of social identities, provides valuable indications of why national efforts to bring an armed conflict to an end and build durable peace should be attentive to civil resistance campaigns.

To start with, the PCSJA case shows that civilians living in the crossfire are not merely passive victims; they can be agents of change. As reflected to some extent in the current peace negotiations in La Havana, peace talks tend to address civilians almost exclusively as victims (the fourth item of the agenda, currently under negotiation, is the

Chapter 6: Conclusion: Lessons from the PCSJA

rights of victims). This of course makes sense since victimization is perhaps the most pervasive form of civilian involvement in war (in Colombia, numbering nearly 6 million victims in the last 50 years). However, there are other ways in which civilians participate in war that are relevant from the perspective of peace policy. The PCSJA case is an illustrative example of civilian agency: civil resistance by ordinary people who turned out to be not merely victims but also, via self-organizing, active nonviolent actors in the conflict.

Intimately related to the previous point, the PCSJA calls attention to the fact that civilians respond differently to war. For example, some people individually decide to leave their lands to avoid violence; actively cooperate with an occupying armed group; still others collectively decide to stay put and mount civil resistance against violence. As we saw in this monograph, war and civilian response to it drastically transformed the preferences and beliefs of San José villagers, their identity, their social, political and organizational forms, and the institutions on which they rely to govern their lives.

These deep transformations should inform policymaking and implementation. For example, San José residents came to hold particular beliefs about the state and its institutions: it was evident from interviews that distrust of the state and the extent to which it lacks legitimacy was a defining feature of the PCSJA mentality. Peace and post-conflict reconstruction policy involves rebuilding state authority throughout national territory, re-legitimizing it and fostering trust in its institutions.

The experience of San José villagers also reveals that during war the state does not exercise authority over its entire territory and population. In fact, mutually exclusive claims to authority and the division of sovereignty are defining aspects of irregular civil war.[110] However, the state's absence does not imply that people live in "black spots" or "ungoverned territories."[111] To be sure, the main competitor to state authority, sovereignty and order are armed groups. Nonetheless, the case examined here shows that organized civilians can also limit or substitute for the lack of state or non-state authority, establishing their own systems of governance. Therefore, detecting and understanding this type of campaign could inform the design and implementation of measures to build peace.

---

[110] See Tilly 1978:191; Kalyvas 2006:18; Wickham-Crowley 1992.
[111] For a detailed treatment of subnational variation in social local order in Colombia see Arjona (forthcoming a). See also Staniland 2012; Mampilly 2011; Arjona, Kasfir, and Mampilly forthcoming.

On the one hand, they enable us to identify areas of the country where the state lacks authority for reasons other than losing them to the control of an armed group. On the other hand, they inform policymakers and implementers about the type of institutions they must deal with or be open to when creating new post-peace agreement stability. If we are to expect San José villagers (as well as other similar resisting communities) to comply with and take part in any new post-conflict common order, interventions need to specifically tackle the lack of trust in the state and integrate functioning grassroots institutions into a new framework.

Finally, the PCSJA case leaves us with an important message regarding the scale at which peace efforts should be advanced. National peace negotiations usually take place between high-level representatives of warring parties, without involving authentic grassroots peacemakers such as the PCSJA. As Landon and Hancock (2012: 161) note, elite-level peacemakers often expect local leaders and communities to act as passive spectators or supporters of their efforts, and might even desire that local initiatives do not "get in the way." Getting communities such as the PCSJA involved and concerned with national peace efforts could help gain the support, cooperation and legitimacy that the implementation of a negotiated peace agreement requires. Instead of seeing these campaigns as potential obstacles, negotiators should see the opportunities that localized processes offer.

National peace negotiations usually take place between high-level representatives of warring parties, without involving authentic grassroots peacemakers such as the PCSJA.

Resisters have created capacity in everyday life, maintained order, produced local legitimacy, and identified needs and how to respond to them. In fact, resisters are well aware of what they can offer to peace-building efforts and therefore might be expecting that their views are taken into account. In both group and individual interviews with leaders of the PCSJA this became apparent: "So I think that the peace that we have been trying to build as a Community in the past 17 years is an example for both the national and international community. We have said no to arms. We have shown that we need no arms to build peace [...] peace is achieved through civil resistance and peaceful life"[112]

---

[112] Interview L(G)/PCSJA#7 25.04.2014

Chapter 6: Conclusion: Lessons from the PCSJA

and "I believe that the Peace Community is like a seed of peace and we need to expand it to many different parts of the country and the world to see whether one day this war is finally over."[113] The PCSJA case, as Lederach (2015) has noted more generally, weighs in favor of on-the-ground dialogue in local areas prior to completing a major peace agreement. This dialogue could help identify security and livelihood challenges that civilians face across Colombia and anticipate nonviolent, civilian-based responses to those challenges.[114]

Although complementarity between national and local processes is not an easy task, some analysts suggest that "the most beneficial time period for the use of complementarity appears to be during the negotiation or implementation of any peace agreement" (Hancock and Mitchell 2012, 176). If this is to be the case, it means that Colombia is at the right stage to discover how grassroots processes such as the PCSJA can be recognized and integrated in the national peace process.

---

[113] Interview L/PCSJA#11 27.04.14

[114] This is happening in other regions of Colombia where communities experienced disproportionate levels of violence during the war. Through an active collaboration with the United Nations Development Programme (UNDP), regular meetings have been held with grassroots, regional, and national leaders in Montes de María, a mountainous region on the northern coast of Colombia. See Lederach (2015).

Cited Literature

Ackerman, Peter, and Jack DuVall. 2000. *A Force More Powerful: A Century of Nonviolent Conflict*. New York: St. Martin's Press.

Adhikari, Prakash. 2012. "The Plight of the Forgotten Ones: Civil War and Forced Migration." *International Studies Quarterly* 56 (3): 590–606.

———. 2013. "Conflict-Induced Displacement, Understanding the Causes of Flight." *American Journal of Political Science* 57 (1): 82–89.

Amnesty International. 2008. "'Leave Us in Peace!' Targeting Civilians in Colombia's Internal Armed Conflict." AI Publications. London: Amnesty International. https://www.amnesty.org/fr/documents/AMR23/023/2008/en/.

Anderson, Mary B., and Marshall Wallace. 2012. *Opting Out of War: Strategies to Prevent Violent Conflict*. Boulder, Colorado: Lynne Rienner Publishers Inc.

Arjona, Ana. forthcoming b. "Resisting Rebel Rulers: Civilian Challenges to Rebel Governance." In *Rebel Governance*, edited by Ana Arjona, Nelson Kasfir, and Zachariah Cherian Mampilly, 280–317. Cambridge: Cambridge University Press.

———. forthcoming a. *Social Order in Civil War*. Cambridge University Press.

———. 2013. "Agency and Governance in the Context of Civil Conflict." Policy Brief 1. Brighton, UK: Institute of Development Studies / Economic & Social Research Council.

Arjona, Ana, Nelson Kasfir, and Zachariah Cherian Mampilly, eds. forthcoming. *Rebel Governance*. Cambridge University Press.

Avruch, Kevin, and Roberto Jose. 2007. "Peace Zones in the Philippines." In *Zones of Peace*, edited by Landon E. Hancock and Christopher Mitchell, 51–70. Bloomfield, CT: Kumarian Press.

Baines, Erin, and Emily Paddon. 2012. "'This Is How We Survived': Civilian Agency and Humanitarian Protection." *Security Dialogue* 43 (3): 231–47.

Balcells, Laia, and Patricia Justino. 2014. "Bridging Micro and Macro Approaches on Civil Wars and Political Violence Issues, Challenges, and the Way Forward." *Journal of Conflict Resolution* 58 (8): 1343–59.

Bartkowski, Maciej J. 2013a. "Recovering Nonviolent History." In *Recovering Nonviolent History: Civil Resistance in Liberation Struggles*, edited by Maciej J. Bartkowski, 1–30. Boulder: Lynne Rienner Publishers Inc.

———. , ed. 2013b. *Recovering Nonviolent History: Civil Resistance in Liberation Struggles*. Boulder: Lynne Rienner Publishers Inc.

Bejarano, Ana María. 1988. "La Violencia Regional Y Sus Protagonistas: El Caso de Urabá." *Análisis Político* 4: 41–68.

Blattman, Christopher, and Edward Miguel. 2010. "Civil War." *Journal of Economic Literature* 48 (1): 3–57.

Bosi, Lorenzo, and Donatella Della Porta. 2012. "Micro-Mobilization into Armed Groups: Ideological, Instrumental and Solidaristic Paths." *Qualitative Sociology* 35 (4): 361–83.

Bosi, Lorenzo, and Stefan Malthaner. 2013. "A Framework to Analyze Forms of Political Violence Based on Patterns of Socio-Spatial Relations." At the European University Institute. Florence, Italy.

Bossert, Silvie. 2010. "Pilgrimage 2010 in Bogotá: Hope for Colombia." Monte do Cerro, Portugal: Tamera. www.tamera.org/political-network/articles/grace-in-colombia-reportz/.

Bouvier, Virginia Marie, ed. 2009. *Colombia: Building Peace in a Time of War*. Washington, D.C.: United States Institute of Peace.

Carroll, Leah Anne. 2011. *Violent Democratization: Social Movements, Elites, and Politics in Colombia's Rural War Zones, 1984-2008*. South Bend: University of Notre Dame Press.

Cederman, Lars-Erik, and Kristian Skrede Gleditsch. 2009. "Introduction to Special Issue on 'Disaggregating Civil War.'" *Journal of Conflict Resolution* 53 (4): 487–95.

Cederman, Professor Lars-Erik, Kristian Skrede Gleditsch, and Halvard Buhaug. 2013. *Inequality, Grievances, and Civil War*. New York: Cambridge University Press.

Chenoweth, Erica, and Kathleen Gallagher Cunningham. 2013. "Understanding Nonviolent Resistance: An Introduction." *Journal of Peace Research* 50 (3): 271–76.

Chenoweth, Erica, and Orion A. Lewis. 2013. "Unpacking Nonviolent Campaigns Introducing the NAVCO 2.0 Dataset." *Journal of Peace Research* 50 (3): 415–23.

Chenoweth, Erica, and Maria J. Stephan. 2011. *Why Civil Resistance Works: The Strategic Logic of Nonviolent Conflict*. New York: Columbia University Press.

CINEP. 2005. "San Jose(sito) de Apartadó. La Otra Versió." Caso Tipo 6. Noche Y Niebla. Bogotá: CINEP.

Degregori, Carlos Ivan. 1999. "Reaping the Whirlwind: The Rondas Campesinas and the Defeat of Sendero Luminoso in Ayacucho." In *Societies of Fear: The Legacy of Civil War, Violence and Terror in Latin America*, edited by Kees Koonings and Dirk

Kruijt, 63–87. London; New York: Zed Books.

Degregori, Carlos Ivan, José Coronel, Ponciano Del Pino, and Orin Starn. 1996. *Las Rondas Campesinas Y La Derrota Del Sendero Luminoso*. 2nd Edition. Lima: IEP Ediciones.

Della Porta, Donatella. 1995. *Social Movements, Political Violence and the State: A Comparative Analysis of Italy and Germany*. New York: Cambridge University Press.

———. 2008. "Research on Social Movements and Political Violence." *Qualitative Sociology* 31 (3): 221–30.

Duyvendak, Jan W., and James M. Jasper, eds. forthcoming. *Breaking Down the State: Protestors Engaged with Authorities*.

Earl, Jennifer. 2003. "Tanks, Tear Gas, and Taxes: Toward a Theory of Movement Repression." *Sociological Theory* 21 (1): 44–68.

———. 2004. "Controlling Protest: New Directions for Research on the Social Control of Protest." *Research in Social Movements, Conflicts and Change* 25: 55–83.

———. 2006. "Introduction: Repression and the Social Control of Protest." *Mobilization* 11 (2): 129–43.

Elster, Jon. 1999. *Alchemies of the Mind: Rationality and the Emotions*. Cambridge, U.K.; New York: Cambridge University Press.

Engel, Stefanie, and Ana María Ibáñez. 2007. "Displacement Due to Violence in Colombia: A Household-Level Analysis." *Economic Development and Cultural Change* 55 (2): 335–65. doi:10.1086/edcc.2007.55.issue-2.

Francis, David J. 2005. *Civil Militia: Africa's Intractable Security Menace?* Aldershot, Hants, England; Burlington, VT: Ashgate.

Fumerton, Mario. 2001. "Rondas Campesinas in the Peruvian Civil War: Peasant Self-Defence Organisations in Ayacucho." *Bulletin of Latin American Research* 20 (4): 470–97.

Gamson, William A, Bruce Fireman, and Steven Rytina. 1982. *Encounters with Unjust Authority*. Homewood, Ill.: Dorsey Press.

Garcia, Ed. 1997. "Filipino Zones of Peace." *Peace Review* 9 (2): 221–24.

Gayer, Laurent. 2012. "Have Gun, Will Travel: Interpreting the Trajectories of Female Irregular Combatants." In *Understanding Collective Political Violence*, edited by Yvan Guichaoua, 105–23. New York: Palgrave Macmillan.

Giraldo, Javier. 2000. "San José de Apartadó: Perfil de Una Comunidad de Paz."

———. 2010. *Fusil O Toga, Toga Y Fusil. El Estado Contral La Comunidad de Paz de San José de Apartadó*. Bogotá: CINEP.

Goldstone, Jack A. forthcoming. "Conclusion: Simplicity vs. Complexity in the Analysis of Social Movements." In *Breaking Down the State: Protestors Engaged with Authorities*, edited by Jan W. Duyvendak and James M. Jasper.

Goldstone, Jack A., and Charles Tilly. 2001. "Threat (and Opportunity): Popular Action and State Response in the Dynamics of Contentious Action." In *Silence and Voice in the Study of Contentious Politics*, edited by Ron Aminzade, Jack A. Goldstone, Doug McAdam, Elizabeth Perry, William Sewell, Sidney G. Tarrow, and Charles Tilly, 179–94. Cambridge: Cambridge University Press.

Goodwin, Jeff. 2012. "Introduction to a Special Issue on Political Violence and Terrorism: Political Violence as Contentious Politics." *Mobilization* 17 (1): 1–5.

Granada, Soledad, Jorge Restrepo, and Alonso Tobón Garcia. 2009. "Neoparamilitarismo En Colombia: Una Herramienta Conceptual Para La Interpretación de Dinámicas Recientes Del Conflicto Armado Colombiano." In *Guerra Y Violencias En Colombia: Herramientas E Interpretaciones*, edited by David Aponte and Jorge Restrepo, 467–500. Bogotá: Pontificia Universidad Javeriana.

Gross, Jan Tomasz. 1979. *Polish Society under German Occupation: The Generalgouvernement*, 1939-1944. Princeton: Princeton University Press.

Gutierrez Sanín, Francisco, and Elisabeth J. Wood. 2014. "What Should We Mean by 'Pattern of Political Violence'? Repertoire, Targeting, Frequency, and Technique." In Washington, D.C.

Hancock, Landon E., and Christopher Mitchell. 2012. "Between Local and National Peace: Complementarity or Conflcit?" In *Local Peacebuilding and National Peace: Interaction between Grassroots and Elite Processes*, edited by Christopher Mitchell and Landon E. Hancock, 161–78. London; New York: Continuum.

Hernandez Delgado, Esperanza. 2004. *Resistencia Civil Artesana de Paz: Experiencias Indigeneas, Afrodescendientes Y Campesinas*. Bogotá: Editorial Pontificia Universidad Javeriana.

Hess, David, and Brian Martin. 2006. "Repression, Backfire, and the Theory of Transformative Events." *Mobilization* 11 (2): 249–67.

Hoffman, Danny. 2004. "The Civilian Target in Sierra Leone and Liberia: Political Power, Military Strategy, and Humanitarian Intervention." *African Affairs* 103 (411): 211–26.

———. 2007. "The Meaning of a Militia: Understanding the Civil Defence Forces of Sierra

Leone." *African Affairs* 106 (425): 639–62. doi:10.1093/afraf/adm054.

Holmes, Robert L, and Barry L. Gan. 2005. *Nonviolence in Theory and Practice*. Long Grove: Waveland Press.

Hultman, Lisa. 2010. "Keeping Peace or Spurring Violence? Unintended Effects of Peace Operations on Violence against Civilians." *Civil Wars* 12 (1-2): 29–46.

Human Rights Watch. 2010. "Paramilitaries' Heirs. The New Face of Violence in Colombia." New York: Human Rights Watch. http://www.hrw.org/sites/default/files/reports/colombia0210webwcover_0.pdf.

Humphreys, Macartan, and Jeremy M. Weinstein. 2008. "Who Fights? The Determinants of Participation in Civil War." *American Journal of Political Science* 52 (2): 436–55.

Ibáñez, Ana María. 2009. "Forced Displacement in Colombia: Magnitude and Causes." *Economics of Peace and Security Journal* 4 (1): 48–54.

Justino, Patricia, Tilman Brück, and Philip Verwimp, eds. 2014. *A Micro-Level Perspective on the Dynamics of Conflict, Violence, and Development*. Oxford: Oxford University Press.

Kalyvas, Stathis N. 2003. "The Ontology of 'Political Violence': Action and Identity in Civil Wars." *Perspectives of Politics* 1 (3): 475–94.

———. 2006. *The Logic of Violence in Civil War*. Cambridge: Cambridge University Press.

———. 2008. "Promises and Pitfalls of an Emerging Research Program: The Microdynamics of Civil War." In *Order, Conflict, and Violence*, edited by Stathis N. Kalyvas, Ian. Shapiro, and Tarek E. Masoud, 397–421. Cambridge: Cambridge University Press.

———. 2012. "Micro-Level Studies of Violence in Civil War: Refining and Extending the Control-Collaboration Model." *Terrorism Polit. Violence Terrorism and Political Violence* 24 (4): 658–68.

Kalyvas, Stathis N., and Ana Arjona. 2005. "Paramilitarismo: Una Perspectiva Teorica." In *El Poder Paramilitar*, edited by Alfredo Rangel. Bogotá: Planeta.

Kalyvas, Stathis N., and Matthew Adam Kocher. 2007. "How 'Free' Is Free Riding in Civil Wars?: Violence, Insurgency, and the Collective Action Problem." *World Politics* 59 (2): 177–216.

Kaplan, Oliver. 2010. "Civilian Autonomy in Civil War." Ph.D. Dissertation, Stanford University. http://purl.stanford.edu/bj965cc7673.

———. 2012. "Shootings and Shamans: Local Civilian Authority Structures and Civil War Violence in Colombia." SSRN Scholarly Paper ID 2102751. Rochester, NY: Social Science Research Network. http://papers.ssrn.com/abstract=2102751.

———. 2013. "Protecting Civilians in Civil War: The Institution of the ATCC in Colombia." *Journal of Peace Research* 50 (3): 351–67.

Kasfir, Nelson. forthcoming. "Rebel Governance — Constructing a Field of Inquiry: Definitions, Scope, Patterns and Causes." In *Rebel Governance*, edited by Ana Arjona, Nelson Kasfir, and Zachariah Mampilly, 6–49. Cambridge University Press.

———. 2005. "Guerrillas and Civilian Participation: The National Resistance Army in Uganda, 1981–86." *The Journal of Modern African Studies* 43 (02): 271–96.

Keck, Margaret E., and Kathryn Sikkink. 1998. *Activists beyond Borders: Advocacy Networks in International Politics*. Ithaca: Cornell University Press.

———. 1999. "Transnational Advocacy Networks in International and Regional Politics." *International Social Science Journal* 51 (159): 89–101.

Koloma Beck, Teresa. 2012. *The Normality of Civil War. Armed Groups and Everyday Life in Angola*. Frankfurt: Campus.

Kuran, Timur. 1995. *Private Truths, Public Lies: The Social Consequences of Preference Falsification*. Cambridge: Harvard University Press.

Lederach, John Paul. 2015. "Colombian Peace Process: Bridging Research and Practice." *Peace Policy*. January 28. http://peacepolicy.nd.edu/2015/01/28/colombian-peace-process-bridging-research-and-practice/.

Lichbach, Mark Irving. 1995. *The Rebel's Dilemma*. Ann Arbor: University of Michigan Press.

Lipsitz, Lewis, and Herbert M. Kritzer. 1975. "Unconventional Approaches to Conflict Resolution: Erikson and Sharp on Nonviolence." *Journal of Conflict Resolution* 19 (4): 713–33.

Lubkemann, Stephen C. 2008. *Culture in Chaos: An Anthropology of the Social Condition in War*. Chicago: University of Chicago Press.

Mahony, Liam. 1997. "Unarmed Bodyguards." *Peace Review* 9 (2): 207–13.

Mampilly, Zachariah Cherian. 2011. *Rebel Rulers: Insurgent Governance and Civilian Life during War*. Ithaca: Cornell University Press.

Martin, Brian. 2006. *Justice Ignited: The Dynamics of Backfire*. Lanham Md.: Rowman & Littlefield Publishers.

Masullo, Juan. In progress. "The Evolution of Noncooperation in Civil War." Doctoral Dissertation, Florence: European University Institute.

———. 2013. "Book Review. Chenoweth, Erica & Maria J. Stephan (2011) *Why Civil Resistance Works. The Strategic Logic of Nonviolent Conflict*. (New York: Columbia University Press)." *Global Policy Journal*.

http://www.globalpolicyjournal.com/blog/29/11/2013/book-review-why-civil-resistance-works-strategic-logic-nonviolent-conflict-erica-che

Masullo, Juan, and Jone Lauzurika. 2014. "Bringing the 'New Wars' Debate Back on Track: Building on Critiques, Identifying Opportunities, and Moving Forward." *Global Policy* 5 (4): 415–24.

McAdam, Doug. 1982. *Political Process and the Development of Black Insurgency*, 1930-1970. Chicago: University of Chicago Press.

McAdam, Doug. 1986. "Recruitment to High-Risk Activism: The Case of Freedom Summer." *American Journal of Sociology* 92 (1): 64–90.

McAdam, Doug., Sidney G. Tarrow, and Charles Tilly. 2001. *Dynamics of Contention*. Cambridge: Cambridge University Press.

Metelits, Claire. 2010. *Inside Insurgency : Violence, Civilians, and Revolutionary Group Behavior*. New York: New York University Press.

Mitchell, Christopher. 2007. "The Theory and Practice of Sancturay. From Asylia to Local Zones of Peace." In *Zones of Peace*, edited by Landon E. Hancock and Christopher Mitchell, 1–18. Bloomfield, CT: Kumarian Press.

Mitchell, Christopher, and Landon E. Hancock. 2007. "Local Zones of Peace and a Theory of Sanctuary." In *Zones of Peace*, edited by Landon E. Hancock and Christopher Mitchell. Bloomfield, CT: Kumarian Press.

Mitchell, Christopher, and Sara Ramírez. 2009. "Local Peace Communities in Colombia. An Initial Comparison of Three Cases." In *Colombia: Building Peace in a Time of War*, edited by Virginia Marie Bouvier, 245–70. Washington, D.C.: United States Institute of Peace.

Mitchell, Christopher, and Catalina Rojas. 2012. "Against the Stream: Colombian Zones of Peace under Democratic Security." In *Local Peacebuilding and National Peace: Interaction between Grassroots and Elite Processes*, edited by Christopher Mitchell and Landon E. Hancock, 39–68. London; New York: Continuum.

Nepstad, Sharon Erickson. 2011. *Nonviolent Revolutions. Civil Resistance in the Late 20th Century*. Oxford: Oxford University Press. http://www.oxfordscholarship.com/view/10.1093/acprof:oso/9780199778201.001.0001/acprof-9780199778201.

Olson, Mancur. 1965. *The Logic of Collective Action: Public Goods and the Theory of Groups*. Cambridge: Harvard University Press.

Pardo, Ruben Dario. 2008. "Peace Community of San José de Apartadó, Colombia: A

Lesson of Resistance, Dignity and Courage." War Resister's International. http://www.wri-irg.org/node/5200.

Perlez, Jane. 1990. "Spared by Rebels? The Spirit Says That'll Be $2." *The New York Times*, August 24. http://www.nytimes.com/1990/08/24/world/mongol-journal-spared-by-rebels-the-spirit-says-that-ll-be-2.html.

Petersen, Roger Dale. 2001. *Resistance and Rebellion. Lessons from Eastern Europe*. Cambridge: Cambridge University Press.

PBI. 2010. "Doce Años de Resistencia Pacífica: La Guerra Sigue." PBI Colombia Special Issue 14. Bogotá: Peace Brigades International. http://www.peacebrigades.org/fileadmin/user_files/projects/colombia/files/colomPBIa/100107_boletin_PBI_desplazamiento_2010_WEB.pdf.

———. 2012. "Comunidad de Paz de San José de Apartadó: 15 Años de Resistencia En Medio Del Conflicto Armado." Online Article. Bogotá: Peace Brigades International. http://www.pbi-colombia.org/field-projects/pbi-colombia/news-from-colombia/news/?tx_ttnews%5Btt_news%5D=3299&cHash=d67c2a6714dd37d6439ccce21963e0e1.

Popkin, Samuel L. 1979. *The Rational Peasant*. Berkeley: University of California Press.

Ramírez Tobón, William. 1993. "Estado Y Crisis Regional: El Caso de Urabá." *Análisis Político* 20: 23–38.

Restrepo, Gloria Inés. 2011. "Memoria E Historia de La Violencia En San Carlos Y Apartadó." *Universitas Humanística* 72 (June-December): 157–88.

Roberts, Adam. 2011. "Introduction." In *Civil Resistance & Power Politics. The Experience of NonViolent Action from Gandhi to the Present*, edited by Adam Roberts and Garton Ash, 1–24. Oxford: Oxford University Press.

Rojas, Catalina. 2007. "Islands in the Stream. A Comparative Analysis of Zones of Peace in Colombia's Civil War." In *Zones of Peace*, edited by Landon E. Hancock and Christopher Mitchell, 71–90. Bloomfield, CT: Kumarian Press.

Romero, Mauricio. 2000. "Changing Identities and Contested Settings: Regional Elites and the Paramilitaries in Colombia." *International Journal of Politics, Culture, and Society* 14 (1): 51–69.

———. 2003. *Paramilitares y Autodefensas, 1982-2003*. Bogotá: Instituto de Estudios Políticos y Relaciones Internacionales.

Sanford, Victoria. 2003. "Peacebuilding in a War Zone: The Case of Colombian Peace Communities." *International Peacekeeping* 10 (2): 107–18.

———. 2004. "Contesting Displacement in Colombia: Citizenship and State Sovereignty at the Margins." In *Anthropology in the Margins of the State*, edited by Veena Das and Deborah Poole. Santa Fe, N.M.; Oxford [England]: School of American Research Press; James Currey.

Santos, Soliman M. 2005. *Peace Zones in the Philippines: Concepts, Policy & Instruments*. Quezon City: Gaston Z. Ortigas Peace Institute in cooperation with the Asia Foundation.

Schock, Kurt. 2003. "Nonviolent Action and Its Misconceptions: Insights for Social Scientists." *PS: Political Science & Politics* 36 (04): 705–12.

———. 2005. *Unarmed Insurrections: People Power Movements In Nondemocracies*. 1st ed. Minneapolis: University of Minnesota Press.

———. 2013. "The Practice and Study of Civil Resistance." *Journal of Peace Research* 50 (3): 277–90.

Scott, James C. 1976. *The Moral Economy of the Peasant. Rebellion and Subsistence in Southeast Asia*. New Haven: Yale University Press.

Semelin, Jacques, Claire Andrieu, and Sarah Gensburger. 2011. *Resisting Genocide: The Multiple Forms of Rescue*. London: C Hurst & Co Publishers Ltd.

Sharp, Gene. 1973. *The Politics of Nonviolent Action*. 3 vols. Boston: Porter-Sargent.

———. 2003. *There Are Realistic Alternatives*. Boston: Albert Einstein Institution.

———. 2005. *Waging Nonviolent Struggle: 20th Century Practice and 21st Century Potential*. Boston: Extending Horizons Books.

Smithey, Lee, and Lester R. Kurtz. 2003. "Parading Persuasions: Nonviolent Collective Action as Discourse in Northern Ireland." *Social Movements, Conflicts, and Change* 24: 319–59.

Staniland, Paul. 2012. "States, Insurgents, and Wartime Political Orders." *Perspectives on Politics* 10 (2): 243–64.

Starn, Orin. 1995. "To Revolt against the Revolution: War and Resistance in Peru's Andes." *Cultural Anthropology* 10 (4): 547–80.

Steele, Abbey. 2009. "Seeking Safety: Avoiding Displacement and Choosing Destinations in Civil Wars." *Journal of Peace Research* 46 (3): 419–29.

———. 2011. "Electing Displacement: Political Cleansing in Apartadó, Colombia." *Journal of Conflict Resolution* 55 (3): 423–45.

Suarez, Andrés Fernando. 2007. *Identidades Políticas Y Exterminio Recíproco: Masacres Y Guerra En Urabá (1991-2001)*. La Carreta Editores. Bogotá.

Svensson, Isak, and Mathilda Lindgren. 2011. "Community and Consent Unarmed Insurrections in Non-Democracies." *European Journal of International Relations* 17 (1): 97–120. doi:10.1177/1354066109350049.

Tarrow, Sidney G. forthcoming. "Contentious Politics." In *Oxford Handbook of Social Movements*, edited by Donatella Della Porta and Mario Diani. Oxford: Oxford University Press.

———. 2007. "Inside Insurgencies: Politics and Violence in an Age of Civil War." *Perspectives on Politics* 5 (03): 587–600. doi:10.1017/S1537592707071575.

———. 2011. Power in Movement. Cambridge: Cambridge University Press.

Tilly, Charles. 1978. *From Mobilization to Revolution*. Reading: Addison-Wesley Pub. Co.

———. 2003. *The Politics of Collective Violence*. Cambridge: Cambridge University Press.

Uribe, Maria Teresa. 2004. "Emancipacion social en un contexto de guerra prolongada. El caso de la Comunidad de Paz de San José de Apartadó." In *Emancipación social y violencia en Colombia*, edited by Boaventura de Sousa Santos and Mauricio García Villegas. Bogotá: Grupo Editorial Norma.

Valenzuela, Pedro. 2009. "Neutrality in Internal Armed Conflicts : Experiences at the Grassroots Level in Colombia." Uppsala: Uppsala Universitet. /z-wcorg/.

Valenzuela, Pedro. 2010. "La neutralidad como estrategia para la protección de la población civil en conflictos armados internos: un estudio de caso." In *Desplazamiento en Colombia : prevenir, asistir, transformar : cooperación internacional e iniciatives locales*, edited by Cristina Churruca and Donny Marteens. Medellín: La Carreta Editores.

Verwimp, Philip, Patricia Justino, and Tilman Brück. 2009. "The Analysis of Conflict: A Micro-Level Perspective." *Journal of Peace Research* 46 (3): 307–14.

Viterna, Jocelyn. 2006. "Pulled, Pushed, and Persuaded: Explaining Women's Mobilization into the Salvadoran Guerrilla Army." *American Journal of Sociology* 112 (1): 1–45. doi:10.1086/ajs.2006.112.issue-1.

———. 2013. *Women in War: The Micro-Processes of Mobilization in El Salvador*. Oxford: Oxford University Press.

Weinstein, Jeremy M. 2007. *Inside Rebellion: The Politics of Insurgent Violence*. Cambridge; New York: Cambridge University Press.

Wickham-Crowley, Timothy P. 1987. "The Rise (And Sometimes Fall) of Guerrilla Governments in Latin America." *Sociological Forum* 2 (3): 473–99.

Wickham-Crowley, Timothy P. 1992. *Guerrillas and Revolution in Latin America: A*

Comparative Study of Insurgents and Regimes since 1956. Princeton: Princeton University Press.

Wilson, Ken B. 1991. "War, Displacement, Social Change and the Re-Creation of Community: An Exploratory Study in Zambezia, Mozambique. Preliminary Report of a Field Study in Milange District March-April 1991." Oxford: Refugee Studies Center. http://repository.forcedmigration.org/../show_metadata.jsp?pid=fmo%3A718.

———. 1992. "Cults of Violence and Counter-Violence in Mozambique." *Journal of Southern African Studies* 18 (3): 527–82.

Wood, Elisabeth J. 2003. *Insurgent Collective Action and Civil War in El Salvador.* Cambridge: Cambridge University Press.

———. 2008a. "The Social Processes of Civil War: The Wartime Transformation of Social Networks." *Annual Review of Political Science* 11: 539–61.

———. 2008b. "The Social Processes of Civil War: The Wartime Transformation of Social Networks." *Annual Review of Political Science* 1 (1): 539–61.

Zarate-Laun, Cecilia. 2012. "Background on San José de Apartadó."http://colombiasupport.net/wp-content/uploads/2012/03/Background-on-San-Jose-de-Apartado1.pdf.

Acronyms

CIJP	Inter-Church Commission for Justice and Peace (commonly referred to by the acronym for its name in Spanish, Comisión Intereclesial de Justicia y Paz)
CINEP	Center for Research and Popular Education
ELN	National Liberation Army (Ejército de Liberación Nacional, or ELN, in Spanish)
EPL	Popular Liberation Army (Ejército Popular de Liberación, or EPL, in Spanish)
FARC	Revolutionary Armed Forces of Colombia (Fuerzas Armadas Revolucionarias de Colombia, or FARC, in Spanish)
FOR	Fellowship of Reconciliation
PBI	Peace Brigades International
PCSJA	Peace Community of San José de Apartadó
NGO	Nongovernmental organization
UNDP	United Nations Development Programme

List of Figures

Fig. 1. Civilian Responses to Civil War 20
Fig. 2. Urabá in National, Regional and World Contexts 24
Fig. 3. Peace Community of San José in National and Regional Contexts 38
Fig. 4. Violent Events by Perpetrator, Apartadó 1989 – 2010 (Including San José) 44
Fig. 5. Civilian Deaths by Perpetrator, Apartadó 1989 – 2010 (Including San José) 45
Fig. 6. Nonviolent Tactics Used by PCSJA by Category 59
Fig. 7. Nonviolent Actions of the PCSJA 60

www.ingramcontent.com/pod-product-compliance
Lightning Source LLC
Chambersburg PA
CBHW040223040426
42333CB00051B/3422